NEWMAN AND FAITH

LOUVAIN THEOLOGICAL & PASTORAL MONOGRAPHS
——————————— 31 ———————————

NEWMAN AND FAITH

edited by

Ian Ker & Terrence Merrigan

PEETERS PRESS
LOUVAIN – PARIS – DUDLEY, MA

W.B. EERDMANS

2004

Library of Congress Cataloging-in-Publication Data

Oxford International Newman Conference (3rd: 2001: Keble College, University of Oxford)
    Newman and faith / edited by Ian Ker & Terrence Merrigan.
      p. cm. -- (Louvain theological & pastoral monographs; 31)
    Includes bibliographical references and index.
    ISBN 90-429-1461-0 (alk. paper)
      1. Newman, John Henry, 1801-1890. I. Ker, I. T. (Jan Turnbull) II. Merrigan, Terrence. III. Title. IV. Series.

BX4705.N5184 2004
230'.2'092--dc22

                                                                    2004044523

© 2004, Peeters, Bondgenotenlaan 153, 3000 Leuven, Belgium

ISBN 90-429-1461-0 (Peeters Leuven)
D. 2004/0602/67

TABLE OF CONTENTS

Preface VII

Antecedent Presumption, Faith, and Logic 1
    D. Z. PHILLIPS

"To Live and Die upon a Dogma": Newman and
Post/Modern Dogma 25
    Gerard LOUGHLIN

Newman and the Particularity of Conscience 53
    Gerard J. HUGHES, SJ

"Historia Veritatis": On Newman's *Essay on the
Development of Christian Doctrine* 75
    Bruno FORTE

Newman on Faith in the Trinity 93
    Terrence MERRIGAN

Newman, Councils, and Vatican II 117
    Ian KER

Dispensations of Grace: Newman on the Sacramental
Mediation of Salvation 143
    Geoffrey WAINWRIGHT

Newman through the Looking Glass 183
    Elisabeth JAY

Notes on Contributors 209

Index of Names 211

Index of Subjects 215

PREFACE

The third Oxford International Newman Conference, held at Keble College, Oxford from 11 to 15 August 2001, celebrated the bicentenary of Newman's birth. The theme of the conference was 'Newman and faith', the subject that was the overriding preoccupation of his life. This volume comprises a selection of the principal papers delivered.

As at the previous two conferences, we had two purposes: first, to seek to address, so far as possible, the different aspects of Newman's writings, the educational, the historical, the literary, the philosophical, the spiritual, and the theological; and second, to relate Newman's work to contemporary concerns and interests in these different disciplines.

In the first paper, D. Z. Phillips considers the fundamental philosophical question of the relation between faith and reason, suggesting that there are four possible readings of Newman's thought. Theologically, Gerard Loughlin proposes a postmodernist reading of Newman 'as a sort of narrativist theologian'. Gerard J. Hughes, SJ insists that Newman's contribution to fundamental moral theology, his celebrated treatment of conscience, must be interpreted in terms of its Aristotelian rather than scholastic background.

Bruno Forte argues that the originality of Newman's theory of doctrinal development lies principally in its union of the ontological, hermeneutic, and ecclesiological dimensions. Terrence Merrigan claims originality for Newman's trinitarian and christological theology because of the novel way he applies his distinction between the notional and the real. Ian Ker discusses Newman's significance as a historical theologian of councils, particularly with regard to the interpretation and meaning of the Second Vatican Council. Geoffrey Wainwright considers Newman's writings on the sacramental mediation of salvation, including his thought on the sacramental principle itself, the Church, Christ, and the particular sacraments.

Finally, from a literary point of view, Elisabeth Jay examines the autobiographical significance of Newman's novel *Callista*, with special reference to the character of Juba.

ANTECEDENT PRESUMPTION, FAITH AND LOGIC

D. Z. PHILLIPS

"All his life John Henry Newman was concerned with how one ought to speak of knowing and believing, reason and faith ... How — and how far — is Christian faith to be justified intellectually?" This is still a living question and Newman's way of handling the question is perhaps of special interest to us today.[1]

So wrote J. M. Cameron in the first of two pioneering, but neglected, essays on Newman written in 1957 and 1960.[2] The difficulty — and it is a philosophical one — is to determine in what way Newman *did* handle the issues Cameron refers to, and why this should be of particular philosophical interest to us today. I am grateful for the invitation to this conference, as a non-specialist in Newman studies. I hope to explore some relations between Newman's thought and certain movements within contemporary philosophy of religion.

Newman accepted the empiricist distinction between proof and probability. Proof belongs to logic and mathematics. These are the realms in which certainty can be achieved; realms which exclude religious belief. In the second half of his *Grammar of Assent*, Ian Ker tells us, Newman faced what he regarded as a major problem: "how is one justified in believing what one cannot prove?"[3]

---

[1] James M. Cameron, "The Logic of the Heart," *The Night Battle* (Baltimore, MD: Helicon Press, 1962) 203.

[2] The second essay is "Newman and Empiricism."

[3] Ian Ker, *John Henry Newman* (Oxford: Oxford University Press, 1988) 642.

Locke criticised Descartes for failing to distinguish between geometric bodies and real bodies. That the sum of the interior angles of a triangle equal 180° is part of what we mean by a triangle. The properties of real bodies, on the other hand, have to be discovered by empirical investigation. We make practical judgements which are not deductive arguments. Referring to our dealings with such matters, Locke said that, for the most part, we live in the twilight of probabilities.

Can faith be understood as the product of assessing probabilities? Richard Swinburne would say so. To believe in God, 51% probability is enough. Would Newman have agreed? William Froude thought he did, and criticised him on the same grounds as I have criticised Swinburne: probability is an inadequate epistemological category to account for the certitude of faith.

James Collins argues that this criticism of Newman is unjustified. It emphasises the influence of empiricism and Butler's analogical reasoning on Newman, but forgets the equal influence of the notion of practical wisdom he found in Aristotle and the Greek Fathers. Newman wanted to extend this notion, showing that it has application, not only in moral matters, but also in scientific, historical and legal reasonings and investigations. If we remember this, Collins argues, we will appreciate that Newman is not using the term "probability" in Locke's sense. For him, it is simply a "catchall" phrase to distinguish all non-deductive forms of reasoning from deductive reasoning. If reasoning is not deductive, it is called probabilistic.[4] No doubt the term may mislead us, but it is more important to concentrate on its use than to quarrel over the label.

One major reason why the use of the term "probability" in Newman's work can be misleading, is that he certainly wanted to

[4] James Collins, "John Henry Newman," *The Encyclopedia of Philosophy*, ed. Paul Edwards (New York: Macmillan Publishing Co. Inc. and The Free Press, 1967) V: 482-483.

emphasise certitudes in the concrete circumstances of human life. This can be seen in the pursuit of intellectual investigations. For example, a pathologist has dissected a relatively small number of skulls. If someone asked, "Are you sure that *every* skull contains a brain?," the pathologist would be extremely puzzled by the question. If he said anything at all it might be, "Of course." The certitude is shown in the fact that the question does not arise.

Newman also emphasised that certitudes are found in practical circumstances where no methodological issues are involved. For example, think of Newman writing his books and sermons in familiar surroundings. Would Newman have been content to say that the existence of those books and sermons, or the presence of his familiar surroundings, were matters of probability? Of course not. Again, the certitude would show itself in the fact that no such question arises.

In religion, too, Newman did not think that certitudes can be replaced with talk of probabilities. He referred to evidentialism, in the manner of Paley, as the "high and dry" party. In his *University Sermons* he speaks of "the age of evidences as 'a time when love was cold'."[5] He made fun of the consequences of substituting probability for the certitudes of faith: "If this were to be allowed, then the celebrated saying, 'O God, if there be a God, save my soul, if I have a soul!' would be the highest measure of devotion: — but who can really pray to a Being, about whose existence he is seriously in doubt?"[6] Newman's words resonated with me, since I had made similar criticisms in my own work.[7]

---

[5] John Henry Newman, *Sermons Chiefly on the Theory of Religious Belief — Preached before the University of Oxford* (1843). Quoted by Cameron in "Newman and Empiricism," 232.

[6] *Apo.*, 19.

[7] See D. Z. Phillips, *Faith After Foundationalism* (Boulder, MO/San Francisco, CA/Oxford: Westview Press, 1995) 10.

As we know, Newman had a term to convey the way we respond to ponderable and imponderable evidences in the context of our concrete modes of reasoning, and the ways in which we reach conclusions there — he called it the illative sense. Even allowing for the fact that Newman is not referring to any kind of esoteric faculty, the term is somewhat of an idle wheel. My reason for saying this can be illustrated by a tension in Collins' remarks on the subject. On the one hand, Collins uses the illative sense to refer to our personal responses within the concrete modes of reasoning in our lives. These reasonings are said to have a common pattern, but all that is meant by "the common pattern" is their non-deductive character. On the other hand, Collins emphasises that when we pay attention to these modes of reasoning, we see that they vary, each having a distinctive character. This applies to religious reasoning as much as to any other. Collins writes, "Whether there is certitude in an act of religious faith cannot be settled by general stipulation about the meaning of probability and the judgement of belief. There must be a direct examination of the particular case and its grounds for claiming something about the order of concrete fact."[8] It is not simply that someone confined to a conception of formal reasoning will not understand religious judgements. It is also the case that someone sound in some forms of concrete reasoning, may be blind to others.

Putting all these considerations together, of how much worth is a term so general as the illative sense? Why not settle for saying, as a prelude to detailed examination, that our discourse and responses to argument and discussion take a variety of forms, and that each case, if it is to be appreciated, must be considered in its particularity?

I want to explore Newman's arguments against this background. I am going to present four readings of aspects of Newman's work,

---

[8] Collins, "John Henry Newman," 483.

more tentatively than my text may suggest. None of these will be free of difficulties and qualifications. I do not pretend to offer final conclusions, but it will be evident from what I say that I think philosophical progress is achieved as we move from reading to reading.

1. Newman and Psychologism

By "psychologism," I mean the tendency to treat logical issues as though they were psychological issues. In wanting to account for certitudes in our concrete modes of reasoning, Newman had to argue that in reaching such conclusions, in an act of assent, the mind goes beyond the probabilistic inferences of Locke. In calling attention to such assent, Newman claimed that he was being more empirical than Locke. What he claimed to have found is said to be of the utmost importance for religious belief. According to Newman, Collins argues, "The religious inquirer uses his mind in much the same way as does the jurist, the historian, and the biologist: all share in a common pattern of inquiry that demands a distinctive and responsible use of intelligence moving in a religion somewhere between formalism and psychologism."[9] Keble had suggested that the object of faith is received with such love and devotion that despite the fact that one is faced only by probabilities, these prove sufficient to create an inner conviction in the mind. Newman did not think that this went to the heart of the problem. In his *University Sermons*, he tried to provide an analysis of this inner conviction in terms of the workings of the mind which result in a mental state called "certitude." Unlike mathematical certitude, which follows immediately from deductive reasonings, religious

---

[9] *Ibid.*, 481.

certitude, faced by probabilities, emerges, via natural tendencies, as a distinctive mental state.

It would be misleading to attribute to Newman the isolated mental self of empiricism which leads, ultimately, to solipsism, and to the unbridgeable sceptical gap between consciousness and reality. Nevertheless, the appeal to certitude as a mental state has been subjected to a logical critique which points to difficulties of which there is little, if any, recognition by Newman. They all involve psychologism. Cameron lists four of them.[10]

First, whatever mental state one calls "certitude," it is logically compatible with the non-existence of the state of affairs, or with the falsity of the proposition, it is said to be certain of. The connection between the mental state and what we normally mean by "certitude" is thus made a psychologically contingent matter. Newman is not grasping the logical issue involved when he responds by saying that the trouble lies, not in the mental certitude, but in the falsity.

Second, if we confuse the internal relations between claims to certitude and the practices within which they are made, we have to fall back on certitude as a mental state which gives its meaning "all at once." Wittgenstein calls this a magical view of sense, one which ignores the practical surroundings in which certainty may be present or arrived at.

Third, Newman claimed that not even the real assent captured in the mental state of certitude guarantees action. Again, this inverts a logical relation. So far from a claim to certitude being separable from behaviour in this psychologistic way, it is logically connected

---

[10] Cameron, "Newman and Empiricism," 241. Powerful examples of the logical critique can be found in Ludwig Wittgenstein, *Philosophical Investigations* (Oxford: Blackwell, 1953) and in John Langshaw Austin, *Sense and Sensibilia* (Oxford: The Clarendon Press, 1962).

to it. If the behaviour of a person is inappropriate, the claim to certitude is overruled no matter what mental state is invoked.

Fourth, if certitude is a private mental state, how can another person know anything about it, or how could two people ever know that they shared the same certitude? On this view, familiar features of our shared certitudes become logical impossibilities.

These four logical difficulties with psychologism cannot be evaded. It seems that Newman is guilty of such evasion when he says in his *Sermons*, "No analysis is subtle and delicate enough to represent adequately the state of mind under which we believe, or the subjects of belief, as they are presented to our thoughts."[11] Cameron is insisting, rightly on my view, that one cannot seek psychological solutions to logical problems; one cannot confuse conceptual relations between certitude and practice, with psychological associations which are contingent. Because Cameron thinks that this psychologism is pervasive in Newman's *Grammar of Assent*, he concludes that that work is overrated philosophically. On the other hand, his general view is that Newman is underrated as a philosopher. To see why, Cameron would say, we have to go beyond the psychologism in Newman's work.

It would be difficult to argue that psychologism is never to be found in Newman. On the other hand, it could be argued that to emphasise it is an ungenerous reading of his work. As we have seen, Newman never tired of emphasising the particular character of our concrete modes of reasoning. Surely, it was never his intention to isolate our certitudes from these contexts. The illative sense is personal, in the sense that it is something a person must exercise for him or her self, but the individual is not the creator of the modes of reasoning in which it is exercised. These modes of reasoning, according to Newman, have their own antecedent presumptions or

[11] John Henry Newman, *Fifteen Sermons Preached Before the University of Oxford* (London: Rivingtons, 1890) 267.

probabilities. These are not probabilities in the normal sense, beyond which we are said, in some way, to arrive at the mental state of certitude — the view which leads to accusations of psychologism. Newman's antecedent presumptions and probabilities are said, not simply to colour evidence, but even to determine what is to count as evidence. He seems to be saying that we always have a certain conception of the world, whether we like it or not. This seems far removed from the view of ourselves in psychologism as solitary consciousnesses set over against the world. Newman insists that we are active beings *in* the world. Indeed, it is this very fact which leads Cameron, the critic of his psychologism, to find, in Newman, a penetrating response to scepticism similar to the response one can find in Hume. In our second reading of Newman, we consider this response.

2. Newman and Negative Apologetics

According to Cameron, Newman shared the conventional view of Hume, among Christians of his day, "as the great infidel philosopher, the most subtly dangerous of the adversaries of the Christian religion." Cameron also argues, however, that Newman "shares with Hume a dramatic and paradoxical interpretation of that empiricist tradition of which they are both ornaments. In both, a destructive philosophical analysis is a moment in an argument designed to show that we have no alternative to putting our trust in 'nature'."[12]

The destructive element in empiricism comes from its fatal, sceptical admission that we cannot step outside our experiences to check whether they correspond to a world independent of ourselves. On the other hand, Hume tells us, our minds are furnished with an instinctive belief in such an independent world. Whether

---

[12] Cameron, "Newman and Empiricism," 223.

he likes it or not, the sceptic shares this belief. As Hume famously remarked, "Nature has not left this to his choice, and has doubtless esteem'd it an affair of too great importance to be trusted to our uncertain reasonings and speculations."[13] Newman wanted to say of our antecedent presumptions what Hume said of our instinctive, natural beliefs, "Nature certainly does give sentence against scepticism."[14] In both cases we have to trust them. This simply goes to show the fundamental role of trust and faith in our lives.

This neat argument depends on a contentious issue in Hume scholarship. Does Hume's category of the mind's natural beliefs include belief in God? If not, can it be extended to include religious belief? Cameron's answer to the first question is "No." His answer to the second question is "Yes," but that Hume would oppose the extension. Natural beliefs in human beings have certain characteristics: they are universal, uniform, and unavoidable. By contrast, Cameron argues, "there are, for Hume, no such good reasons, there is no happy coincidence of natural propensity and rational hypothesis, when questions connected with philosophical theology come to be considered."[15] While some philosophers argue that Hume's "true religion" is a minimal natural belief in a God who is responsible for the universe, most contemporary philosophers of religion concur with Cameron's conclusions.[16]

---

[13] David Hume, *A Treatise of Human Nature*, ed. Peter H. Nidditch (Oxford: The Clarendon Press, 1978) 187.

[14] John Henry Newman, *Tracts Theological and Ecclesiastical*, no. 85, 72.

[15] Cameron, "Newman and Empiricism," 229.

[16] For the view that Hume includes belief in God among our fundamental beliefs see H. O. Mounce, *Hume's Naturalism* (London/New York: Routledge, 1999). For the contrary view see J. C. A. Gaskin, *Hume's Philosophy of Religion* (London: Macmillan, 1988); Terence Penelhum, "Natural Belief and Religious Belief in Hume's Philosophy," *Philosophical Quarterly*, 33 (1983) 166-181; Keith E. Yandell, *Hume's Inexplicable Mystery: His Views on Religion* (Philadelphia, PA: Temple University Press, 1990).

But has Hume the right to exclude belief in God from the category of natural beliefs? Cameron argues that he does not, and that Newman has an argument to show why this is so. Newman argues that Hume cannot produce independent criteria for what is to count as an object of fundamental faith and trust. What we accept as criteria, Newman argues, is itself determined by our antecedent presumptions. These presumptions in turn, Cameron argues, "in Hume's case (and no doubt in Newman's too) ... [are] at least in part shaped by temperament and by the cultural milieu within which he moved most happily."[17] In this way, belief in God is said to be on a par, epistemologically, with belief in the existence of physical bodies, and no philosophical argument can show otherwise.

This argument is similar to that employed in early versions of contemporary Reformed epistemology, where the motivation, like Newman's, is religious. In both cases there is a resistance to secular rationalism's claim to determine the perspectives in which a fundamental faith can be expressed. After all, the claim that these perspectives are limited to those secular rationalism is prepared to admit, is not itself a fundamental belief. To claim otherwise would be to be guilty of what the postmodernist Lyotard called the tyranny of metanarrative.[18] Lyotard was influenced by Wittgenstein, who said that the tendency to make one perspective the paradigm for all others is the result of a craving for generality, or the result of a one-sided diet of examples.

Whether we are considering Newman or Reformed epistemology, assent to belief in God is said to be given by those disposed to accept the Christian perspective and the style of argument to be found within it. It is not an assent to be expected from

---

[17] Cameron, "Newman and Empiricism," 229.

[18] See Jean-François Lyotard, *The Postmodern Condition* (Minneapolis, MN: University of Minnesota Press, 1991).

any human being by virtue of a rationality said to be independent of all antecedent presumptions. Thus, believers cannot show non-believers, on neutral grounds, why they should adopt the antecedent presumptions of Christianity. On the other hand, non-believers cannot, on neutral grounds, show Christians that they are irrational to do so. We seem to have a classic case of negative apologetics. Newman seems to be an example of it when he says of his belief in transubstantiation, "But for myself, I cannot indeed provide it, I cannot tell *how* it is; but I say, 'Why should it not be? What's to hinder it?'."[19]

There is an obvious disquiet about this kind of negative apologetics. It seems to lead to an open-door epistemology in which *anything* could be adopted as an antecedent presumption. Reformed epistemology had to face this objection when asked why belief in a Great Pumpkin could not be a basic belief. Alvin Plantinga replied, "We must assemble examples of beliefs and conditions such that the former are properly basic in the latter, and examples of beliefs and conditions such that the former are *not* properly basic in the latter."[20] I responded, "Notice, beliefs and *conditions*. These conditions are our practices. We do not have a choice about where to look. Without appeal to these conditions, Plantinga could not appeal to what is or what is not 'properly basic', since it is within our practices that the notions of 'obviousness' and 'what is proper' have their purchase."[21] The same could be said of Newman's antecedent presumptions. They cannot be the determinants of practice, since it is in our practices that such presumptions have their

---

[19] *Apo.*, 239.

[20] Alvin Plantinga, "Reason and Belief in God," in *Faith and Rationality*, ed. Alvin Plantinga and Nicholas Wolterstorff (Notre Dame, IN: University of Notre Dame Press, 1983) 76.

[21] Philips, *Faith After Foundationalism*, 28.

status. Strictly speaking, they cannot be the *antecedents* of our practices, since it is the practices which hold them fast.

Once again, however, it might be argued that a more generous
reading of Newman would rescue him from the difficulties of negative apologetics, as it rescued him from the difficulties of psychologism. We need to recall, once more, Newman's insistence on
our concrete modes of reasoning. It could then be argued that, just
as Newman does not isolate certitude, as a mental state, from these
modes of reasoning, so he does not isolate our presumptions from
them. To establish such an argument, we need to take a closer look
at the relation between so-called antecedent presumptions and practices. This will be the topic of the third and fourth readings of
Newman's work.

3. Newman and Epistemological Naturalism

At the end of the introductory section of my paper, I questioned the
usefulness of the notion of the illative sense. I asked whether we
should not settle for giving conceptual attention to the various
forms of our discourse with each other. There are tendencies in
philosophy which stand in the way of such attention, some of which
can be found in Newman's work. I want to concentrate on those
which are the results of an epistemological naturalism to be found
in Hume, but which is found in its most developed forms in the philosophy of Thomas Reid and the Scottish naturalists.

Many commentators on Hume have argued that he is being ironic
when he seems to commend religious believers for their dependence on faith. Hume's real position, it is said, is to condemn the
irrationality of religious believers for such dependence. Mounce
argues that this "is an absurd interpretation, since it is in conflict
with Hume's whole philosophy. On Hume's view, none of us can
prove our fundamental beliefs. Reason is impotent without belief

to sustain it. It would be an evident inconsistency on his part to condemn the Christians for not proving theirs."[22]

On this view, our forms of discourse become objects of faith and trust. Faith and trust about what? Presumably, faith that our forms of discourse do put us into contact with reality. Hume attacks popular apologetics, Mounce argues, precisely because it looks for proof. Hume, on the other hand, embraces the orthodoxy of the primacy of faith. Newman embraces this orthodoxy: "... we must begin with believing, and ... conviction will follow; that as for the reasons for believing, they are for the most part implicit, and but slightly recognized by the mind that is under their influence; that they consist moreover rather of presumptions and guesses, ventures after the truth than of accurate proofs; and that probable arguments are sufficient for conclusions which we even embrace as most certain, and turn to the most important uses. On the other hand, it has ever been the heretical principle to prefer Reason to Faith, and to hold that things must be considered true only so far as they are proved."[23]

But Newman, it seems, makes wider epistemic claims. According to this reading of Newman, the primacy of faith over reason is not simply a feature of religious belief. The primacy of faith is characteristic of our epistemic relation to *all* our fundamental beliefs, whether it be belief in God, or belief in physical objects. With the aid of quotations from Newman, Ker sums up the wider epistemic claims as follows:

> However "full" and "precise" the "grounds" and however systematic our method, however clear and tangible our evidence, yet when our argument is traced down to its simple elements, there must be something assumed ultimately which is incapable proof. Faith, then,

[22] H.O. Mounce, *Hume's Naturalism* (London: Routledge, 1999) 107.

[23] John Henry Newman, *An Essay on the Development of Christian Doctrine* (London: Longmans, Green & Co., 1949) 343.

is no different from other kinds of intellectual activity where "we must assume something to prove anything, and can gain nothing without a venture." Indeed, the more important the knowledge is, the more subtle is "the evidence on which it is received" — "We are so constituted, that we insist upon being sure as is conceivable, in every step of our course, we must be content to creep along the ground, and can never soar." And just as "Reason with its greatest conclusions, is confessedly a higher instrument than Sense with its secure premisses, so Faith rises above Reason, in its subject-matter, more than it falls below it in the obscurity of its process."[24]

Anyone wanting to embrace epistemological naturalism has to face four difficulties at least, two within the notion itself, and two which show how epistemological naturalism confuses logical and epistemological views.

The first difficulty has to do with our epistemic relation to the world. If Newman wants to teach us epistemic modesty about our being in the world, and to deny the sceptic's request for proof to show we *know* that fact, all well and good. But how much better off are we if we say that we believe that we are in the world, and that this is a matter of faith? The sceptic will still ask, with good reason, for a justification of that belief or faith.

The second difficulty arises from an attempt to answer the sceptic's question. It is admitted that we cannot prove our fundamental beliefs. Our attitude towards them, it is said, is not to regard them as guilty until proved innocent, but to regard them as innocent until proved guilty. Moreover, this attitude is rational since it is based on the practical success afforded us by our fundamental beliefs in our dealings with the world.[25] Here we find echoes of Newman's evocation of practical wisdom and judgement. Wittgenstein has

[24] Ker, *John Henry Newman*, 261. The quotations are from Newman's *Fifteen Sermons*.

[25] For such a view see William P. Alston, *Perceiving God* (Ithaca, NY: Cornell University Press, 1991). For my criticisms, see *Faith After Foundationalism*.

shown that this response has the appearance of providing a practical justification without, in fact, being one:

"'But isn't it experience that teaches us to judge like *this*, that is to say, that it is correct to judge like this?' But how does experience *teach* us, then? *We* may derive it from experience, but experience does not direct us to derive anything from experience. If it is the *ground* of our judging like this, and not just the cause, still we do not have a ground for seeing this in turn as a ground. No, experience is not the ground for our game of judging. Nor is it its outstanding success."[26]

The third difficulty has to do with calling our modes of concrete reasoning *antecedent* beliefs. Mounce admits that, normally, people do not reason at all about our fundamental beliefs, such as belief in an independent world. He admits that when philosophers have reasoned about them, this has often resulted in confusion. But Mounce persists in calling them beliefs.[27] But is belief in an independent world an *antecedent* belief at all? We do not sit on chairs, climb stairs, fill buckets, eat apples, because we have an antecedent belief in an independent world. On the contrary, any talk of an independent world is held fast by such activities. Moreover, it is by reference to them that we try to get the sceptic to see that he cannot mean what he says when he denies the reality of an independent world. Such an argument should appeal to Newman who, as we have seen, says that nature certainly gives sentence against scepticism.

The fourth difficulty questions the logical propriety of dealing with our modes of reasoning as though they were objects of belief. We entertain beliefs within certain contexts, such as science or religion, but these contexts are not beliefs. To think otherwise would

[26] Ludwig Wittgenstein, *On Certainty* (Oxford: Blackwell, 1979) paras. 130-131.
[27] Mounce, *Hume's Naturalism*, 103-104.

have curious consequences. For example, people may have conflicting scientific or religious beliefs, but since the conflicting
beliefs are scientific and religious, we'd have to conclude that people who have beliefs which, in the ordinary sense of "belief" are
diametrically opposed, share, in fact, the same belief! This is the
result of treating the conceptual contexts of our beliefs as though
they were beliefs.

These logical difficulties result from a failure to distinguish
between two uses of "reality." When we ask whether a specific
scientific or religious judgement corresponds to reality, this is simply another way of asking whether the judgement is true or false.
But when the sceptic questions the reality of science or religion,
what is at stake is the intelligibility of science and religion. Eluci-
dating the intelligibility of these practices will include, of course,
how judgements of truth and falsity are made within them. But philosophy is not itself a means by which the substantive judgements
are arrived at, or by which their truth or falsity is determined. Philosophy cannot determine whether there is a chair in a room, or
whether the doctrine of the Real Presence is true.

The distinctions between two uses of "reality" leads to questions about the nature of Newman's work. Is Newman concerned
with the truth of falsity of specific Christian beliefs, or with the
reality, that is, the intelligibility, of the Christian faith? If the
answer is "Both," was he always careful to distinguish between
them? To further these issues we need to turn to our fourth reading of Newman.

4. Newman and World Pictures

Wittgenstein, like Newman, emphasised the variety of our concrete modes of reasoning. He, too, emphasised that in these reasonings, there are matters which are not questioned, matters which

simply do not arise. In *On Certainty*, he asks us to consider someone who claims to have been on the moon, but who considers any
question about how he got there as irrelevant. The person simply
says that he knows when he gets there. Wittgenstein says that we
would feel intellectually very distinct from such a person. We
want to ask certain questions. If someone says they are not relevant, we are nonplussed. If these are not relevant, what could
"relevance" mean? It does not follow that we can prove that
the questions are relevant. Newman is right on that issue. We
would not know how to question them. They are part of what
Wittgenstein calls our world-picture. But they cannot be called, as
Newman calls them, the *presumptions* of our way of thinking and
acting. Rather they are what is involved *in* our way of thinking.
We do not see certain questions as relevant *because* we have a
world-picture. Our world picture *is* treating them as relevant.
A scientist is not enabled to conduct experiments by virtue of
having a world-picture. Conducting experiments in the way he
does *is* his world-picture.[28] I do not see that anything of importance would be lost if Newman's observations on antecedent presumptions were to be re-expressed in these terms, and much
would be gained.

Newman is concerned with the intellectual justification of a
Christian world-picture. This means that he is concerned to eluci-
date the kind of sense it has. He is concerned to show that science
does not have the sole prerogative on reality. What science tells us
about reality is seen in what scientists find out. To appreciate what
is meant by spiritual realities, we need to turn to religious world-
pictures. Newman is anxious that those areas of human life, which

---

[28] For a discussion of these issues see Rush Rhees, *Wittgenstein's "On Certainty:" There Like Our Life*, ed. with an Afterword by D. Z. Phillips (Oxford:
Blackwell, 2003).

involve what he calls "the logic of the heart," should be recognised philosophically. Cameron directs our attention to two examples which contribute to that end. In the first example, Newman warns us against thinking that belief in God is a theoretical belief.

"When we are not personally concerned, even the highest evidence does not move us; when we are concerned the very slightest is enough. Though we know for certain that the planet Jupiter were in flames, we should go on as usual; whereas even the confused cry of fire at night raises us from our beds. Action is the criterion of true faith, as determining accurately whether we connect the thought of God with the thought of ourselves, whether we love Him, or regard Him otherwise than we regard the existence of the solar system."

In the second example, Newman is emphasising that belief in the soul, too, is a spiritual matter: "Indeed, it is a very difficult thing to bring home to us; and to feel that we have souls; and there cannot be a more fatal mistake than to suppose we see what the doctrine means, as soon as we can use the worlds which signify it. So great a thing is it to understand that we have souls, that the knowing it, taken in connexion with its results, is all one with *being serious*, i.e., truly religious. To discern our immortality is necessarily connected with fear and trembling repentance, in the case of every Christian."[29]

I am suggesting that Newman's concern with what he called the antecedent presumptions of the Christian faith can be brought into a fruitful relation with Wittgenstein's notion of a world-picture. If we understand the latter notion, we will realise that it makes no sense to ask whether world-pictures correspond to reality. *It is*

[29] Quoted in Cameron, "Newman and Empiricism," 242-243. The quotations are from John Henry Newman, *The Via Media of the Anglican Church*, 2 vols. (New York: Longmans, Green & Co., 1923) 1:105-106; *Parochial and Plain Sermons*, 8 vols. (London: Rivingtons, 1902), 1:19-20.

important not to confuse a world-picture with a picture of the world. A world-picture is not a hypothesis, but a conception of the world in which people come into contact with realities. Distinctions between the real and the unreal, of different kinds, are found within world-pictures. To look for a context-free conception of reality is to look for a confused metaphysical transcendentalism. Wittgenstein says that God himself could tell us nothing about it. We are not reporting, as Reid thinks in his philosophy, on the epistemic limits of our mortal faculties. We are talking, rather, of a logical confusion. This is missed if we say, with Ker, "For logic cannot prove the first principles which it assumes."[30] That does sound like a limitation, whereas to search for the logicality of logic is as confused as seeking a grounding for Newman's concrete modes of reasoning. I prefer the Ker who also says that Newman insists that reason is not an art or a skill, but a spontaneous energy which expresses itself in various forms in our lives.[31] Wittgenstein says that our language-games are unpredictable, and that they are there like our life. It is a philosophical superstition to think that something called "the structure of the world" determines them. We have a scientific interest in the world. It is a philosophical superstition to say that we *must* have had that interest. Primitive peoples wondered at the world. It is a philosophical superstition to say that they *had* to.

There are important differences, of course, between what goes unquestioned in our dealings with our empirical surroundings, and what is fundamental in belief in God. If someone could convince me now that I am not reading this paper in an Oxford that I know quite well, but that I am at home with my family, or in Claremont, California, I would not say I had made a mistake. I'd think I was going crazy, since all my yardsticks would be falling apart. This

---

[30] Ker, *John Henry Newman*, 645.
[31] *Ibid.*, 263.

cannot be said of the loss of religious belief. On the other hand, Newman recognises that a loss of faith is not like a change of opinion within a perspective, but is, rather, the loss of a whole perspective. He says, "Ten thousand difficulties do not make one doubt."[32] Religious belief asks real assent from believers, which is a matter of a life lived in faith, the product of grace, not argument. That is why the essentials of faith can be possessed by the most uneducated person.

Thus far, I have been concerned with Newman's discussion of the sense of Christianity. But Newman wants to discuss, not simply assent to sense, but also assent to truth. Certain aspects of what he says about the latter assent, however, do not accord well, in all respects, with what I have said in the course of my argument. In conclusion, I want to note some of them, ending with those which have a bearing on the nature of philosophical enquiry.

First, Newman argues that real assent is a response of the will to a concrete image of God, rather than an assent to propositions. While I agree with the general direction of this comment, is the way it is expressed a return to the psychologism we have already criticised? It would be if it entails the untenable view of an image which guarantees the response to itself. On the other hand, Newman also says that not even real assent guarantees action. But, then, how is this to be reconciled with his insistence on the active, not theoretical, character of belief in God?

Second, there are times when Newman does speak as though belief in God has a theoretical grounding, albeit one emanating from human experience. I have in mind his analysis of conscience, and his claim that its structure implies a connection, whether it is recognised or not, with belief in God. As Cameron says, Newman

---

[32] John Henry Newman, *Apologia pro Vita Sua* (London: Longmans, Green & Co., 1904) 239.

wants the connection to be conceptual, not merely psychological.[33] Cameron cannot see how it can be, since there is no contradiction in asserting conscience, and denying God. Collins, on the other hand, argues that Newman's argument depends on the characteristics of the structure of conscience.[34] The arguments, however, are weak.

First, conscience is said to be intentional. It points beyond a person to a lawgiver. This first characteristic simply begs the question. Second, conscience is said to be personal, so allowing a real assent to God. But this possibility is not strong enough to give Newman the conceptual conception he needs. Third, the practical orientation of conscience is said to call for practical action, not abstract speculation. But that can be said of the role of conscience in different moralities. In fact, the whole argument depends on the fact that Newman, like Hume, believed in a *consensus humani* in moral matters. Once we recognize the heterogeneity of morals, as we must, philosophically, the whole argument collapses. I would say that what Newman succeeds in presenting is not a proof of faith from conscience, but a conception of conscience from the perspective of faith.

Third, there are times when Newman wants to link religious doctrines to even wider philosophical ambitions. According to Ker, for Newman, there is no philosophy without system,[35] and his system is sacramental. What is "system"? According to Newman, "It is the power of referring every thing to its true place in the universal system ... It makes every thing lead to everything else; it communicates the image of the whole body to every separate member, till the whole becomes in imagination like a spirit, everywhere pervading and penetrating its component parts, and giving them one

---

[33] Cameron, "The Logic of the Heart," 214ff.

[34] Collins, "John Henry Newman," 484.

[35] See Ker, *John Henry Newman*, 265.

definite meaning."[36] What is a sacramental system? It is "the doctrine that material phenomena are both the types and the instruments of real things unseen."[37] What is the status of this claim? It is not the same as the claim that a physical body is, in fact, the product of a hidden designer. In that claim, there is an external relation between the body and the method by which the designer is discovered. To say that the world is God's, on the other hand, is *already* a religious reaction to it. As Collins says, "Newman refused to grant independent value to the design argument which he regarded as a supplementary way of looking at nature on the part of those who already accept God on other grounds."[38] This raises a question: by "philosophy," in this context, does Newman mean simply the religious world-picture, within which, of course everything will be pervaded by a common spirit? If so, "the universality" is within the world-picture. It is not, then, a universal system to which all philosophers should assent. If, however, the latter claim is being made, how is it to be reconciled with Newman's recognition of the variety of our concrete modes of reasoning which cannot be reduced to a system?

Surely, what actually confronts us in our culture is a hubbub of voices to which philosophy has to do conceptual justice. These cannot be seen as parts of a system. That is not the way they bear on each other. They bear on each other in a way more like the bearings parts of a conversation have on each other.[39] One may look at these bearings in the context of the state of a culture at any given time. One may look at the form such bearings take in the life

---

[36] John Henry Newman, *Fifteen Sermons Preached Before the University of Oxford* (London: Longmans, Green & Co., 1918) 291.

[37] Newman, *Apo*logia, 18.

[38] Collins, "John Henry Newman," 484.

[39] See Rush Rhees, *Wittgenstein and the Possibility of Discourse*, ed. D. Z. Phillips (Cambridge: Cambridge University Press, 1998).

of an individual. The relation of an individual to the culture may be harmonious or discordant. What I want to insist on is that these bearings, in whichever context, are not subject to the dictates of philosophy.

Where does Newman stand on such issues? Is there a way of reconciling Ker's claim that, for Newman, there is no philosophy without system, and Collins' insistence on Newman's realism in recognising that a culture is a battlefield in which different perspectives engage with each other?[40] The matter seems complex. Collins points out that Newman had criteria for what is to count as healthy and sick development in a culture. He also points out that the criteria are influenced by Newman's theological views. These considerations would lead one to think that "system" is to be identified with "religious world-picture." On the other hand, Collins also argues that Newman's attention to the cultural battlefield "indicates the wider significance of his study of the dynamics of human thought and institutional forms."[41] By this "wider significance" Collins means a "theory of development." If we ask what *kind* of theory we are referring to here, we are back with our original set of questions about the nature of philosophical enquiry. At this point, I must leave the question open, with respect to Newman, by simply noting that the notion of a *general* theory of development is problematic.

As far as my own view is concerned, I recall how Socrates argued against the Sophists, who wanted to deny any distinction between healthy and sick discourse. Socrates insisted *that* there is a distinction to be drawn, but did not proceed to say, in the name of philosophy, *how* it is to be drawn. Philosophy should argue against any attempt to deny *that* there is a distinction between sickness and health in a culture, but it cannot determine *how* that distinction should be drawn. What one movement regards as a healthy

---

[40] Collins, "John Henry Newman," 485.
[41] *Ibid.*

development, another movement may regard as sick. We need only think of different reactions to the possible demise of religion.

It follows from what I have said that philosophy cannot dictate to theology, although, for philosophical reasons, it may comment on the claims it makes. Newman provides us with a reason why this should be so. He says, "To write theology is like dancing on the tight rope some hundred feet from the ground. It is hard to keep from falling, and the fall is great."[42] Wittgenstein wrote, "An honest religious thinker is like a tightrope walker. He almost looks as if he were walking on nothing but air. His support is the slenderest imaginable. And yet it really is possible to walk on it."[43] If my four readings of Newman's work, relating it to psychologism, negative apologetics, epistemological naturalism, and world-pictures show us anything, it is that there is as much disagreement in our day, as in his, as to what it takes to fall off that tightrope, or to walk on it.[44]

---

[42] Quoted in Ker, *John Henry Newman*, 589.

[43] Ludwig Wittgenstein, *Culture and Value* (Oxford: Blackwell, 1984) 73.

[44] I am grateful to my Claremont colleague, Anselm Min, for his comments on an earlier draft of my paper, which helped me to retract some injudicious claims. This does not imply, of course, that he agrees with my revisions.

"TO LIVE AND DIE UPON A DOGMA"
NEWMAN AND POST/MODERN FAITH

Gerard LOUGHLIN

Today, as in his own day, John Henry Newman (1801-1890) is a contested site, the name for different ways of being Catholic. Competing views of Catholicity still seek for legitimacy by appealing to the authority of Newman's thought, of his intellect, and, not least, his Cardinal's red hat, conferred on him by Pope Pius XIII in 1879.[1] At the beginning of the last century, those known as Liberal Catholics or Catholic Modernists appealed to Newman as their patron saint. George Tyrrell (1861-1909) declared himself a "devout disciple of Newman,"[2] and confessed to having been "brought into, and kept in, the Church by the influence of Cardinal Newman and of the mystical theology of the Fathers and of the Saints."[3] Today, however, it is not Catholic Modernism, but religious postmodernism that might be in want of Newman's *imprimatur*.

Professor Terry Wright, for example, has recently suggested that Newman's reading of the Bible offers a *via media* to postmodernity.[4]

---

[1] For an account see Ian Ker, *John Henry Newman: A Biography* (Oxford: Oxford University Press 1990) 715-723.

[2] Tyrrell to Wilfred Ward, 22 September 1898; quoted in Nicholas Sagovsky, *"On God's Side:" A Life of George Tyrrell* (Oxford: Clarendon Press, 1990) 85.

[3] Tyrrell to Bishop Amigo of Southwark; quoted in M. D. Petre, *The Life of George Tyrrell 1884-1909* (London: Edward Arnold, 1902) 342; and in Sagovsky, *"On God's Side,"* 228.

[4] T. R. Wright, "Newman on the Bible: A Via Media to Postmodernity?," *Newman and the Word*, eds. Terrence Merrigan and Ian T. Ker (Louvain: Peeters Press, 2000) 211-249.

For Newman recognised the "multiplicity of meanings" to which a critical, open and historical reading of the Bible gives rise.[5] "The All-wise, All-knowing God cannot speak without meaning many things at once," Newman declared.

> Every word of His is full of instruction, looking many ways; and though it is not often given to us to know these various senses, and we are not at liberty to attempt lightly to imagine them, yet, as far as they are told us, and as far as we may reasonably infer them, we must thankfully accept them. Look at Christ's words, and this same characteristic will strike you; whatever He says is fruitful in meaning, and refers to many things.[6]

This is of course a perfectly traditional, medieval and patristic, point of view; the Church Fathers having inherited the ancient Greek practice of allegorising any significant religious text. However, it was less common in Newman's day, when the modern interest in a strictly historical reading of the scriptural texts had restricted their meaning to the intentions of their human authors.[7]

It is in Newman's insistence on the several senses of scripture, and in his sensitivity to scripture's indeterminacies and hermeneutical *lacunae*, that Terry Wright finds Newman a proto-Derridean, for whom the meaning of any text is always unstable, a momentary anchorage against the drift of metaphor that affects even the most strictly regulated of discourses. Thus Newman could welcome the power of language to capture our imaginations, while aware of its dangerous imprecision, its always falling short of what we

---

[5] Wright, "Newman on the Bible," 211-212.

[6] John Henry Newman, "The Resurrection of the Body," *Parochial and Plain Sermons* (San Francisco, CA: Ignatius Press, 1997) 174-180, 174.

[7] See Gerard Loughlin, *Telling God's Story: Bible, Church and Narrative Theology* (Cambridge: Cambridge University Press, 1999) 120-132.

attempt to say when we speak of God's word.[8] If we want Newman's confirmation of such a view of language in general, and the scriptures in particular, then, as Wright shows, it is not hard to find. But of course not everyone will welcome such a reading, either of Newman or of the Bible.

William Philbin, writing in 1945, warned that Newman greatly exaggerated the prominence of the allegorical mode of interpretation in patristic times, and omitted to "mention the excesses to which it led many of the Fathers."[9] Philbin is commenting on Newman's *Essay on the Development of Christian Doctrine* (1845), and is keen to demonstrate Newman's distance from the Catholic Modernist heresy. When Newman locates the justification for many ecclesial developments, especially regarding the papacy, in the mystical rather than the literal sense of scripture, he is in danger of casting doubt on the authenticity of these developments. For then they are not properly grounded in the literal, bedrock sense of the scriptures, but in the vagaries of spiritual discernment. Philbin is quick to reassure us that Newman's appeal to the mystical meaning of scripture is just Newman's way of referring to the Church's tradition, which is simply the logical working out of what is always already there in the texts, rather than, as Catholic Modernism might suppose, the expression of the church's changing intimations of the Christian "idea."[10] Yet Philbin's anxiety points to the always tendentious and to be tested nature of Bible reading. It also helps to make the point that Newman is suspect of modernism or postmodernism because he is also medieval, patristic, ancient; what,

---

[8] Wright, "Newman on the Bible," 248-249.

[9] William J. Philbin, "*The Essay on Development*," *A Tribute to Newman: Essays on Aspects of His Life and Thought*, ed. Michael Tierney (Dublin: Browne and Nolan Limited, 1945) 116-143, 138.

[10] Philbin, "The *Essay on Development*," 139.

today, some would call "radically orthodox."[11] And it is the idea that Newman is open to the modern and the postmodern because his theological imagination was open to the premodern, that is advocated in this essay.

Modernism

Accounts of the modern and its cult, modernism, are various. For some the modern world arrives in the eighteenth century with the industrial revolution, while for others it begins in the seventeenth century with the scientific revolution occasioned by Copernicus, Kepler, Galileo and Newton. Some trace it farther back, to the sixteenth century and the Protestant Reformation, to the religious revolution that, according to Max Weber, inaugurated the capitalist ethic. If we think of the modern as not so much a period as a mode of cultural sensibility, we may trace its emergence back to St. Augustine and his *Confessions*, and what many see as the birth of the modern "self" in Augustine's interrogation of his own actions and character.

The modern is the idea that humanity is the maker of its own destiny, of progress toward technological and social utopia. Newton produced the idea of constructing clear and powerful models of the world's working. He provided a paradigm for scientific precision and success. Everyone who came after him wanted to be the Newton of his or her own chosen field. He modelled the stars; Darwin modelled the species; Marx modelled society; and Freud modelled the mind. Others followed. Ferdinand de Saussure modelled language and Claude Lévi-Strauss modelled myth. Above all, there

---

[11] Not, I think, "neo-orthodox," as Wright suggests ("Newman and the Bible," 222), since that might be thought to indicate a connection with the Reformed neo-orthodoxy of Karl Barth. See further *Radical Orthodoxy: A New Theology*, ed. John Milbank, Catherine Pickstock and Graham Ward (London: Routledge, 1999).

was Hegel and his story of the world as the self-realisation of Spirit. In the modern moment, in the mind of the European philosopher, Spirit achieves consummation in a moment of perfect modelling or story telling — telling the world as it truly is. The modern is thus imbued with a great sense of its own importance, of its ability to comprehend the world and make it new. In this it is spurred on by its ability to transform the material environment through technology, and through commerce the matrix of society.

It is this confidence in human endeavour that is also the mark of modernism in theology. Strangely, the apogee of theological modernism was already attained at its inception, in the work of Ludwig Feuerbach (1804-1872).[12] Strangely, because after Feuerbach, modernism would retreat to the halfway position of liberal theology, and it would not be until well into the twentieth century — when, for many, modernism was becoming postmodernism — that Feuerbach's thought would make a significant return, though now with a Nietzschean inflection. The 1960s witnessed "secular" and "death of God" theology (Thomas J. J. Altizer, Paul Van Buren), and the 1980s produced the avowedly postmodern theology of people like Mark C. Taylor in the United States of America and Don Cupitt and the "Sea of Faith" movement in the United Kingdom.

Feuerbach, in his most famous and important work, *The Essence of Christianity* (1841), had inverted Hegel's account of history as the dialectical development of absolute Spirit, arguing that it was Spirit that expressed the development of nature, of human self-understanding. In the works of the religious imagination we see the

---

[12] According to John Milbank, William Warburton (1698-1779) had already outlined all the "analyses of Feuerbach, Marx and Freud concerning such phenomena as projection, displacement, alienation, reification and class conflict." See John Milbank, *The Word Made Strange: Theology, Language, Culture* (Oxford: Blackwell, 1999) 59. A more famous progenitor is of course David Hume (1711-1776) and his *Natural History of Religion* (1757).

"objectification" (*Vergegenständlichung*) or "projection" of human ideals. But in casting such values as love, wisdom and justice into the heavens, humanity is alienated from its true being, and it is the work of the philosopher to return men and women to authenticity by disabusing them of their religious illusions. Borrowing a term from the postmodern lexicon, we can say that Feuerbach sought to "deconstruct" rather than to destroy religion; he sought to show how it worked, and what was valuable in its working. Through religion, and above all the Christian religion, human beings imagine their own perfection, and so begin their own perfecting.

Liberal theology — Protestant and Catholic — is Feuerbachian when it emphasizes the social and subjective dynamics of religion, the cultural contexts in which its stories, symbols and rites are formed, and the ways in which these humanly constructed objectivities rebound upon their makers, influencing the cultural milieu from which they are born and by which they are supported. But liberal theology resists Feuerbach to the extent that it insists upon a still persisting transcendence, which though culturally mediated, is nevertheless beyond both culture and subjectivity. There are of course many versions of such a theological stance, and what makes for the liberal version, is the extent to which a theology supposes the transcendent to be the wager or supposition of a religious culture, as opposed to thinking religion a wager of the transcendent, the means by which the Other draws near. In short, theology is liberal to the extent that it accepts something like the Kantian division between the phenomenal world that we know and the noumenal world that we cannot know but may, or even must, postulate. Furthermore, and most importantly, theology is liberal when it accepts the hegemony of certain scientific methodologies that claim a universal applicability, due to their supposed neutrality regarding all metaphysics; best fitted for investigating a world judged entirely mechanical in its operations.

To some extent, Catholic Modernism fits this rough sketch of liberal theology, since Modernist theologians were greatly influenced by historical biblical criticism, which treated the scriptures as contingent testimonies, requiring a supposedly neutral investigation. Furthermore, they were of the view that religion was the product of human imagination, even if a product that gave unto transcendent reality. Above all, the Modernists sought not to oppose other forms of knowledge, but to integrate them with that of the Church, even though, as their opponents stressed, the Church's knowledge was to be put to the test of these other cognitions, and, more importantly, their methodologies. To the extent that the Modernists looked for an integration of religious and secular knowledge we might suppose them deeply Catholic, but to the extent that the religious was made subservient to the secular, we might suppose them liberals, and, for some, even to allow the distinction of "religious" and "secular" is already to have betrayed an underlying liberalism.

That Newman might be thought modern in the sense thus outlined can seem purely paradoxical, since Newman, if anyone, surely resisted putting the dogmas of the faith to the test of an impartial, secular reason? Newman was famously a defender of the dogmatic principle against the "anti-dogmatic principle" of liberalism, and on this he claimed never to have wavered. "From the age of fifteen, dogma has been the fundamental principle of my religion: I know no other religion; I cannot enter into the idea of any other sort of religion; religion, as a mere sentiment is to me a dream and a mockery."[13] Newman claims to have witnessed in his own lifetime the expansion of liberalism from being the name of a religious faction or party in the Church of England, to its encompassing all of educated society; the development of human reason into the "deep,

---

[13] *Apo.*, 54.

plausible scepticism ... practically exercised by the natural man."[14]
Yet we know that several of the Catholic Modernists in particular,
and many avowed liberals in general, looked to Newman for a modern Catholicism.

The liberal Catholic and biographer of Newman, Wilfred Ward
(1856-1916), looked to Newman for an interpretation of what had
befallen the Church with the declaration of papal infallibility in 1870,
and sought Newman's authority for the legitimate freedom of Catholic
scholarship to engage with non-Catholic thought. "To show the richness of life which she showed in the Middle Ages," Ward declared,
"the Church must have the same opportunities which she had then.
She must be able safely and freely to hold intercourse with secular culture."[15] Like Ward, George Tyrrell found in Newman's stress on the
ultimate inviolability and responsibility of the individual's conscience,
space for a legitimate resistance to forms of church governance that
had little respect for the governed.[16] In Newman's *Essay on the Development of Christian Doctrine*, Tyrrell learned the necessity of doctrinal development for the appearance of eternal truth in a changing
world. Tyrrell was later to hold that Newman's *Essay* failed to think
through the nature of the "deposit of faith," and thus did not really
attain to liberal theology.[17] But it was Newman's work that enabled
Tyrrell to develop his view that the Christian "idea," while unstatable
in itself, is that for which the Church must seek in each Age.[18]

[14] *Apo.*, 234.

[15] Wilfred Ward, *The Life and Times of Cardinal Wiseman*, 2 vols. (London,
1897) II: 581; quoted in Sagovsky, *"On God's Side,"* 83.

[16] See John Henry Newman, *Letter to the Duke of Norfolk*, 1875: "If I am
obliged to bring religion into after-dinner toasts which indeed does not seem quite
the thing I shall drink — to the Pope if you please — still, to Conscience first,
and to the Pope afterwards."

[17] See Sagovsky, *"On God's Side,"* 176.

[18] George Tyrrell, "The Mind of the Church," *The Month* 96 (1900) 125-142;
see Sagovsky, *"On God's Side,"* 110-115.

For those antipathetic to the Modernist spirit, Newman was always suspect; after all, he was, like George Tyrrell, a convert from Protestantism, which taught, above all else, the independence of the individual in matters of faith.[19] One may think Modernism the heresy of heresies, or, on the other hand, a sane and sensible development of Catholic thought, that erred only in being, as Mrs Wilfred Ward put it, in the title of her novel on Modernism, *Out of Due Time* (1906). But there can be little argument that Newman's work leant itself to the Modernist cause, whether or not Newman himself would have approved of such a use. One might say that Newman's style allows for that multiplicity of interpretation that, according to Terry Wright, Newman found in the scriptures.

Thus in so far as Newman's work is open to a Modernist interpretation, it is open to a postmodernist reading. This is of course to suggest a certain continuity between modern and postmodern, that the latter is not so much a radical rupture of the former, as the former's intensification. The argument will be that postmodernism presses further the modern insight into the historically contingent and culturally specific nature of all human endeavours. Modern thought first saw this most clearly with regard to domains like the religious, supposing there to be other areas where such contingency was not operative; but postmodernism sees the ubiquity of the contingent and cultural, so that all pretence to a culture-free, positivist domain, must be abandoned. Thus neither science, nor its subject, the self-contained and autonomous rational neutral observer, is spared the effects of temporality, of his or her utterly human location. Postmodernism is the realisation that all forms of life — including the most rationalistic — depend upon an always prior

---

[19] See Désiré Joseph Mercier, "Lettre Pastorale et Mandement et Carême," 1908, translated in George Tyrrell, *Medievalism: A Reply to Cardinal Mercier* (London: Longmans, Green and Co., 1908) 1-21, 7-9.

belief. As Newman noted, "almost all we do, every day of our
lives, is on trust, i.e. *faith*."[20]

Postmodernism[21]

Jean-François Lyotard has told us that postmodernism is what happens when master stories lose their appeal and become incredible.[22]
A master story or grand narrative is a tale that comprehends everything, telling us not only how things are, but also how they were
and will be, and our place among them. Such stories tell us who
we are. Religious stories are often said to be like this. The Christian story of Creation, Fall and Redemption places the individual
soul within a divine drama of human possibility, of salvation or
damnation. The advent of modernism did not so much end as transform this story. Instead of God's redeemed creation, Marxism
placed us within the unfolding dialectic of history; Darwinism
wrote us into the epic of evolution; and Freud located us in the
theatre of the psyche. Cosmology wants to tell us how the world
began and how it will end.

When modern master stories are avowedly political they are
decidedly utopian; they tell us that society will be better under their
narration. Such stories are always true because they make the world

---

[20] John Henry Newman, "Religious Faith Rational," *Parochial and Plain
Sermons*, 123-130, 125.

[21] In this and the following section I partly quote from one of my earlier works,
where an extended discussion of postmodernism and postmodern theology can be
found. See Loughlin, *Telling God's Story*, 3-26, 29-33. See also Gerard Loughlin,
"The Basis and Authority of Doctrine," *The Cambridge Companion to Christian
Doctrine*, ed. Colin Gunton (Cambridge: Cambridge University Press, 1997) 41-64.

[22] Jean-François Lyotard, *The Postmodern Condition: A Report on Knowledge*,
trans. Geoff Bennington and Brian Massumi (Manchester: Manchester University Press, [1979] 1984).

fit the narrative. We can be characters within them because we can be mastered by them, and it would seem that most of us want to be within such a story; we want to be mastered or written into a narrative that is larger, longer and stronger than our own. This is because stories are secure places. We know how they begin and end. "Once upon a time ... happily ever after." But what happens when these stories break down, when their narrators lose the plot and forget what comes next?

When the grand narratives of religion began to lose their credibility, the modern world was invented by retelling the old stories in a new way. Forgetting about God, people told stories about history, evolution, the psyche, about stars and scientific progress, about genetic manipulation and a master race: about human emancipation through enlightenment and "technoscience." However, these stories also have now become incredible, undesirable, horrible. Now it seems that there are no master stories left, not because they have ceased to be told, but because no one story is dominant, and all jostle for prominence. Through competition with one another, they have been reduced to the level of partial, pragmatic, passing stories, providing the material from which each consumer must now make up his or her own story; and this, so the story goes, is something to be welcomed and celebrated. It is the free-market of self-creation.

We are now happy postmoderns! We are each our own storyteller, living among the ruins of former grand narratives. We tell stories purely for pleasure. Today we tell one story and tomorrow we will tell another. Stories are fashionable; we change them with the seasons, as we change our clothes. Perhaps because this is a relatively new game, we make our stories out of the rubble of the old narratives, the bits and pieces that are lying around, ready to hand. We mix and match, liking the fun of spotting from where the bits have come. Our novels and films are full of quotes and

allusions; our buildings are a little classical, a little rococo, a little
gothic, and even, sometimes a little modernist. Our religions are
new age and neo-pagan, a spiritual smörgåsbord.[23] Our values and
morals are equally multifarious, equally changeable, commodities
like everything else. Alasdair MacIntyre has made a career out of
lamenting the passing of a once stable and coherent tradition of
virtuous habits.[24] But even if such a tradition ever existed outside
of a series of philosophical and theological texts, its disappear-
ance doesn't matter, because now, as perhaps always before, we
get by with what Jeffrey Stout has called a bricolage of ethical
values and moral sentiments. Coherence is not a postmodern
virtue.[25]

Now that the once feared and powerful master narrative of emancipation through state socialism has ceased to be told with any conviction, and the space for the telling of many little stories — the
market of the free world — is being constantly extended, the age
of the master narrative seems finally finished. The announced passing of modernity — and socialism was nothing if not modern —
heralds the end of a world subject to a dominant code, a system ren-
dering all life identical. We have entered a more hospitable, plural
world, an unsystematic domain that no one can be against.

However, there are those who contend that the telling of many
little stories is itself dependent on a rather larger tale, one that cannot be so easily controverted as those it has replaced, because dis-
sembled as the space in which all the little stories are told, as telling
itself. Thus, as Terry Eagleton and others proclaim, postmodern

---

[23] See Paul Heelas, *The New Age Movement: The Celebration of the Self and
the Sacralization of Modernity* (Oxford: Blackwell, 1996).

[24] Alasdair MacIntyre, *After Virtue: A Study in Moral Theory* (London:
Duckworth, [1981] 1985).

[25] Jeffrey Stout, *Ethics After Babel: The Languages of Morals and Their Dis-
contents* (Cambridge: James Clark & Co, 1988).

society — or late capitalist society — is a tyrannous space of freedom, at once "libertarian and authoritarian, hedonist and repressive, multiple and monolithic." While consumer capitalism encourages all manner of possibilities, "restlessly transgressing boundaries and pitching diverse life forms together," unafraid of their inconsistency and contradiction, it nevertheless requires the stable and unimpeded flow of capital and the regular incitement of want, with cycles of surfeit and recess.[26] Eagleton insists that it is no good setting diversity against uniformity, plurality against univocity, seeking to undermine the latter by the former, for the former are already in the service of the latter: "difference, transgressiveness and multiplicity ... are as native to capitalism as cherry pie is to the Land of the Free."[27] The delirium of free-market consumerism is made possible by the iron fist of capitalist technoscience that brooks no dissenters.

Writers like Eagleton and Lyotard point to a fundamental contradiction in the postmodern condition understood as the globalizing culture of late capitalism. For this is a culture that everywhere celebrates the autonomous self, freely choosing its own destiny, that promotes the authenticity of indigenous, home-grown products and homespun philosophies, and yet is supported by global networks of information and capital flow. Viewed positively, this is the irony of global systems thriving through support of local identities, producing the "glocal." Viewed negatively, it is the commodification of anything and everything, to the point where each object or activity becomes equally worthless because only valued within the global system of exchange. Therefore every choice is permitted just as long as it doesn't interfere with the working of the whole, and

---

[26] Terry Eagleton, "Discourse and Discos: Theory in the Space between Culture and Capitalism," *The Times Literary Supplement* 15 July 1994: 3-4, 4.

[27] *Ibid.*, 4.

all choices are indifferent because choice itself is the only index of freedom and value. This is why shopping is now the major form of Western religion, and there is nothing for which one cannot shop — on the internet.[28]

This is to offer an account of the postmodern as a cultural condition, a social phenomenon that developed toward the end of the twentieth century in many, if not most parts of the world, and, if not actually global, aspires to that condition. It is an account that, variously detailed and nuanced, can be found in much social theory, and as such differs from accounts of the postmodern offered in literary and philosophical writing, which has been more interested in questions of "language," "knowledge" and "truth." However, both approaches — the social and the philosophical — have a shared interest in the condition of the subject, understood as an utterly material and textual reality, produced within natural and cultural systems that may be viewed from the perspectives of the physical and political sciences, from the point of view of economics, sociology and philosophy. What locks together the subject in postmodernity with the postmodern discipline that seeks to understand that subject, is the belief that both are already inseparably implicated within one another. For postmodernism, it is no longer possible to think that there is an absolute divide between the knower and the known, subject and object, because both exist only as they are mediated within a reality that is, as postmoderns like to say, always already textual, always already given over to the "word." Epistemology is now understood to be always already ontology. Or, to put the point another way, it is now not only sociology, but all forms of knowledge that are self-reflexive, so that what is known is changed in and through that knowing, because mediated

---

[28] See Steven Spielberg's film *A.I. Artificial Intelligence*, USA 2001, for the dream that even love can be manufactured and mass produced.

within a common sociality. As it was famously put by Jacques Derrida, there is nothing outside the text, no outside text (*il n'y a pas de hors-texte*).[29]

Postmodern Theology

Christian theology has responded to postmodernism in several ways. Some theologians are hostile, others curious, and others extremely enthusiastic, declaring themselves to be postmodern theologians. Of those who are, or have been, enthusiastic over the advent of postmodernism, some, like Mark C. Taylor and Don Cupitt, are inheritors of Feuerbach's projectionism, but filtered through Nietzsche, and, above all, Derrida. They might be called nihilist textualist theologians. The other group of enthusiasts — enthusiastic for at least some postmodern themes — might be called orthodox narrativist theologians, and are people like George A. Lindbeck and John Milbank.[30]

Mark C. Taylor came to prominence with his book *Erring: A Postmodern A/Theology* (1984). It is an accomplished celebration of deferral, of the way in which meaning is always one step ahead of the signs in which we seek it. For Taylor, language is like a vast and endless maze, in which we are forever running, turning this way and that, but never finding a centre or an exit. We never find God, self or meaning, for they are dispersed throughout the labyrinth, noticeable by their absence. Don Cupitt, who announced that he was *Taking Leave of God* in 1980, went on to provide a brilliant if at times hasty manifesto for nihilist postmodern theology.

[29] Jacques Derrida, *Of Grammatology*, trans. Gayatri Chakravorty Spivak (Baltimore, MD: Johns Hopkins University Press, [1967] 1976) 158.

[30] Loughlin, *Telling God's Story*, 10. See further Gavin Hyman, *The Predicament of Postmodern Theology: Radical Orthodoxy or Nihilist Textualism?* (Westminster: John Knox Press, 2001).

He believes that the old certainties have been dispersed across the surface of language. There are no longer any heights or depths, only a cultural skin of endlessly proliferating signs on which we must lightly tread, like *The Long-Legged Fly* (1987). In such a situation, religious values, like all values, have to be created out of nothing through the telling of stories, through make-believe.[31]

For both Taylor and Cupitt postmodernity is welcome and irreversible, and for both of them it has to do with the radical textuality of reality. Both of them are deeply influenced by twentieth-century philosophies of language; by structuralism, post-structuralism and deconstructionism. Both Taylor and Cupitt believe that Christian faith and practice must adopt the new postmodern understanding of the human condition. Cupitt, especially, champions a new sort of Christianity. "We want a new religion that makes liberation and bliss out of the way the world is ... for a beliefless world that is rightly beliefless, we'll need a beliefless religion."[32]

This blissfully beliefless religion is textualism, or, as Cupitt calls it, "culturalism" — the flowing together of language and world as a sea of signs in which we float and swim and have our being.[33] The basic idea of textualism can be grasped by looking up the meaning of a word in a dictionary. You want to find the meaning of the word, but all you find are other words, other signs. Meaning is not outside, but wholly inside language. This does not mean that there is nothing except language in the world. When I hit my foot against a stone it is not a word that causes my pain. But "foot," "stone" and "pain" are all signs. If the world is to have meaning

---

[31] See Mark C. Taylor, *Erring: A Postmodern A/Theology* (Chicago, IL: University of Chicago Press, 1984); Don Cupitt, *Taking Leave of God* (London: SCM Press, 1980) and Don Cupitt, *The Long-Legged Fly: A Theology of Language and Desire* (London: SCM Press, 1987).

[32] Don Cupitt, *The Time Being* (London: SCM Press, 1992) 117.

[33] Cupitt, *Time Being*, 64.

for me, it must come into language, into meaningful being.[34] It must be placed under a description, categorised and indexed. Without language I would hit my foot against a stone and feel pain, but I would not know what I had done, or that I was "hurting," though I might cry out, for the event would be painful but without meaning, for I would be without language. "When I seem to see red," Cupitt writes, "I am already interpreting what I see, for I am classifying it. I am seeing it through a word. And unless I see through words I don't see at all."[35]

Story and narrative have become fashionable topoi for theology, and Cupitt takes to them with relish. Everything is a story, for stories produce every significant thing. Stories produce desire. They manipulate and channel our emotions, directing them toward objects we might otherwise find unexciting. Stories produce reality, establishing certain orders and relations between things and people and between them and other people. They establish the significance of age and gender, of skin colour, class and accent: of all the things that matter and that could be otherwise, if told in a different story. Narratives produce time, the positioning of things before and after, the placing of the present at the complex intersection of individual and communal time-narratives. And stories produce us, our sense of self-hood, of being an "I" with a past and a future, a narrative trajectory.

Religion, needless to say, is also a product of narrative. For Cupitt, it is only a story, but an important one, for the religious story provides our lives with significance; it inspires moral endeavour and conquers the Void. In the past we thought that God wrote

---

[34] Arguably this is also the view of Thomas Aquinas in *De principiis naturae*; but for Thomas, unlike Cupitt, being *demands* entry into language, and this being is not a Kantian unknown or worse, the effloresence of a Nietzschean void.

[35] Cupitt, *Time Being*, 56.

the story, but now we know that we ourselves have written God. Now the religious task is to keep up the fiction, and not with a heavy but with a light touch. We must be "cheerfully fictionalist."[36] For the heavy hand produces a master story that weighs upon the soul. Instead we must be "continually improvising, retelling, embroidering, making it up as we go along."[37]

For textualist theologians such as Taylor or Cupitt, "God" is also a sign; one which, like any other, depends for its meaning on all the rest. God is not outside language, in a place where meaning and truth are self-present, for language has no outside. God is wholly inside language, make-believe like everything else. God is language; the play of signs upon the Void.

> The Void is just movement, change. Semiosis, signification, is a temporal moving process ... Just reading a sentence, we should be able to feel on our pulses the way life and meaning continually come out of the Void and return into it. That's the new religious object. That's what we have to learn to say yes to ... life's urgent transience ... The sign is our only metaphysics, our little bit of transcendence.[38]

The chief problem with textualist theology is that it is not textualist enough. It tells us that there are only stories, but it tends to obscure the fact that in that case, textualism also is only a story; and it is not a Christian story, but a nihilist one, since for textualism it is the story of "formlessness" that goes all the way down. For textualist theology we tell stories against the Void. There is nothing beyond our stories except white noise. This, after Feuerbach and Nietzsche, is its master story: that finally there is only nothing. For Cupitt, religious stories are told to keep the darkness at bay, until the night comes.

---

[36] Don Cupitt, *What is a Story?* (London: SCM Press, 1991) 96.
[37] *Ibid.*, 154.
[38] *Ibid.*, 95.

But we may wonder if there are not some other, better stories, ones that are less complacent about contemporary society, less pessimistic about the human condition, more hopeful of change? For the theologians to whom I now turn, the old ecclesial story of God's self-gift in Christ and Church is such a better story, since, in the telling it looks for the coming of the dawn. This is the story told by those theologians I am calling narrativists, of whom George A. Lindbeck and John Milbank are good examples. They are narrativists because, like the textualists, they accept the ubiquity of language. They believe that our sense of the world is formed by the socially constructed discourses in which we find ourselves, and to which we contribute. We are embedded in language, as is language in us. There is a reciprocal relation between story and storyteller. As I recount my life-story, my story produces the "I" which tells it. I narrate the story by which I am told. And since I am part of a larger community — one in which other people tell stories about me, just as I tell stories about them — I am the product of many inter-related narratives, as is everyone else.

Narrativists also believe that stories go all the way down; our deepest convictions about the world and ourselves are constituted in stories only. As such, stories are human constructions, socially enacted. When the stories that society tells about itself change, so does society. When we change our stories about the world, the world itself changes. However, narrativists, unlike textualists, believe that what matters in story-telling is not the telling itself, but the stories told, the particular narratives unfolded. They are concerned not so much with the fictionality of the world, as with the particular world fictioned. Thus Lindbeck and Milbank are both orthodox theologians because they believe that the Christian story of Christ and his Church is preferable to all others. It is a story to live by.

In 1984 George Lindbeck published a short, powerful and provocative study on *The Nature of Doctrine*. In the book he sought to outline an ecumenical theory of doctrine as the neutral "grammar" of varied Christian discourses. Lindbeck can be read as articulating Wittgenstein's remark that "Grammar tells us what kind of object anything is. (Theology as grammar)."[39] This idea is not original to Wittgenstein, having been suggested in 1901 by Harold Fielding-Hall (1859-1917): "the creeds are the grammar of religion, they are to religion what grammar is to speech."[40] Lindbeck, however, finds a more ancient provenance for creed as grammar in St. Athanasius. Following Bernard Lonergan (1904-85), Lindbeck argues that Athanasius had learned from Greek philosophy how to formulate propositions about propositions, and understood the credal doctrine of the "consubstantiality" of Father and Son as expressing the rule that "whatever is said of the Father is said of the Son, except that the Son is not the Father (*eadem de Filio quae de Patre dicunter exceptio Patris Nomine*)."[41] For Athanasius the doctrine of Nicaea was a second-order rule for Christian speech, and to accept the doctrine meant agreeing to speak in a certain way.

The rule theory of doctrine is not uncontested, and certain related ambiguities and tensions need to be clarified. Firstly, it should be noted that while doctrines are understood as second-order propositions referring to other propositions, symbols and stories, they can also be taken as first-order propositions concerning worldly entities and divine mysteries. Lindbeck insists that a "doctrinal statement

[39] Ludwig Wittgenstein, *Philosophical Investigations*, trans. G. E. M. Anscombe (Oxford: Basil Blackwell, [1952] ²1958) section 371.

[40] H[arold] Fielding[-Hall], *The Hearts of Men* (London: Hurst and Blackett, 1901) 313.

[41] George A. Lindbeck, *The Nature of Doctrine: Religion and Theology in a Postliberal Age* (London: SPCK, 1984) 94. See also Bernard Lonergan, *De Deo Trino* (Rome: Gregorian University Press, 1964) partly translated by C. O'Donovan as *The Way to Nicea* (London: Darton, Longman and Todd, 1976); and Bernard Lonergan, *Method in Theology* (London: Darton, Longman and Todd, 1972) 307.

may also function symbolically or as a first-order proposition." But when it does so, the statement is no longer functioning as a "church doctrine."[42] The doctrinal character of the statement is constituted by its grammatical use.

Secondly, doctrine construed as ecclesial grammar is intimately dependent upon that which it rules: the telling of the story. Doctrine is always secondary to that which it informs — the church's performance of the gospel — which is alone its basis or foundation. Doctrine rests upon nothing other than the Church's telling of Christ's charitable practices, heeding the command to "follow," to do as he does; in short, upon the ecclesial tradition of discipleship. There is thus no legitimation of doctrine, in history or experience, outside of Christian practice itself.

While doctrine is secondary, it is at the same time creatively dependent upon churchly discourse and practice, a constitutive factor in the speech and performance of the Church. Fielding-Hall thought that doctrines were wholly descriptive, being to religion as grammar is to speech. "Words are the expression of our wants; grammar is the theory formed afterwards. Speech never proceeded from grammar, but the reverse. As speech progresses and changes from unknown causes, grammar must follow."[43] Yet grammar can also be understood prescriptively, as setting forth the rules for well-formed speech; and this is how the doctrinal grammar of theology must be understood, as not just describing but as prescribing the proper ordering of story and symbol, praise and prayer.

The canonical scriptures provide the basic narratives for how the Church imagines the world and herself in the world. The Church

[42] Lindbeck, *Nature of Doctrine*, 80.
[43] Fielding-Hall, *Hearts of Men*, 313.

imagines herself within the narrative-world of the Bible, a written-world into which people can be "inscribed." Rather than under-standing the Bible in worldly terms, the Christian understands the world in biblical ones; the Christian takes the biblical narratives, above all the narratives of Christ, as the fundamental story by which all others are to be understood, including his or her own story. "The cross is not to be viewed as a figurative representation of suffering nor the messianic Kingdom viewed as a symbol for hope in the future; rather, suffering should be cruciform, and hopes for the future messianic."[44] The biblically formed narratives of Christ and his Church become the story that literally makes the world; it goes all the way down.

On Lindbeck's postliberal view, language and story come first, world and experience second. We only recognise the world as world because we can say "world." Experience occurs within language. All that we have has been given in words. This is much the same as textualism. But where narrativist theology differs is in its master story. Whereas for textualist nihilism it is the movement of signs upon the surface of the Void, for Lindbeck it is the story of Christ and his Church. One could say that the difference between these stories is the difference between Nothing and Everything, between ultimate darkness and hoped-for dawn, between violence and har-mony. This last way of stating the difference is after John Milbank, who made the difference between malign and benign postmodernism a theme of his magisterial study, *Theology and Social Theory* (1990).

On Milbank's account, Christianity is postmodern because it is not founded on anything other than the performance of its story. It cannot be established against nihilism by reason, but only pre-sented as a radical alternative, as something else altogether. It is also postmodern because its story — God's story — imagines a

---

[44] Lindbeck, *Nature of Doctrine*, 118.

world "out of nothing," as opposed to the chaos, the void of nihilism. God's world is one of true "becoming," in which people are not fixed essences but life-narratives with a future. The story of Jesus Christ gives to the Church a pattern for peaceful existence. It is an "atoning" peace of mutual forgiveness and the bearing of one another's burdens. This peace is sought in the nomadic city of the Church, an open-ended tradition of charity, of "differences in community."[45]

From the point of view of Christian theology, narrativist orthodoxy would seem preferable to textualist nihilism, but many argue that what plagues the latter also affects the former. Firstly, is it possible to affirm God while allowing that such an affirmation can take place only within a story, albeit a master story which is said to go all the way down, without remainder? Cupitt believes that any talk of the transcendent, of that which is beyond or outside language, is rendered "silly" by the fact that it is talk, and thus wholly within language.[46] If God appears in a story — as he does in the Bible — God must appear as a human-like, gendered and speaking character, with ideas and assumptions appropriate to the time of his appearing, with feelings and intentions, "behaving in general like an extra-powerful and demanding king."[47] He will be all too human. And isn't it odd that people can write about him, as if from God's point of view? Who was around when God made the heaven and the earth, to tell us about it? The whole thing is human artifice.

However, we can use words to talk about things other than words, and we can use words obliquely, metaphorically, analogically. Talk of God is not easy, but nor is it impossible. Thus in

---

[45] John Milbank, *Theology and Social Theory: Beyond Secular Reason* (Oxford: Basil Blackwell, 1990) 417.

[46] Cupitt, *Time Being*, 90.

[47] Cupitt, *What is a Story?*, 114.

response to Cupitt, narrativist theology, while agreeing that God is a human-like character in the biblical narrative, nevertheless insists that God is not a human being. Of course the first story of Genesis is narrated from an impossible standpoint, it is a work of imagination after all. But this does not mean that it is a false depiction of the world as creation. Narrativist theology turns to the tradition of negative theology, which, while it insists on the unknowability of God, also insists that God's self-saying, above all in Jesus Christ, allows us to speak of God, even if we still do not know of what we speak when we speak of God.[48]

Truth is said to be a problem for narrativism. How can there be true stories when it is said that there are only stories? For it is supposed by many that a true story is one that matches up to reality, to the way things are (a correspondence theory of truth). But if the way things are can never be known, because all we can know are stories of one sort or another, we can never match stories against reality, but only against one another. Thus it is said that even science is not so much about the matching of scientific theories against reality, as the matching of theories against experimental data, observation statements and so forth, which are always already theory-laden. Science matches theory-stories against observation-narratives (a coherentist theory of truth).

Whatever the case with science, narrative postmodern theology insists that Christian truth has never been a matter of matching stories against reality. It has always been a matter of matching reality-stories against the truth: Jesus Christ. For the Christian Church it has always been a life-story that comes first, against which all other things are to be matched. This life-story is what "truth" means in Christianity. Nor is this a matter of making up the truth,

---

[48] See Graham Ward, *Barth, Derrida and the Language of Theology* (Cambridge: Cambridge University Press, 1995).

because it is the truth that makes up the story. The story is imagined for Christians before it is re-imagined by them: the story is given to the Church. That, at any rate, is the Church's story.

Of course, the foregoing is a circular argument, and it is not possible to point to the giving of the story other than from within the story, which must already be underway for the gift to appear. Thus the gift can only be recognised in its reception, and in that moment recognised as already given. All attempts at an apology for the Church's story can only be *ad hoc* responses to alternative narratives, attempts to show that they also are already implicated in Christ's story, and so already constituted by a gift they have yet to recognise.

It is said that narrativist theology renders the Church sectarian. For it denies that reason provides an autonomous language in which everything can be discussed; rather it supposes a multiplicity of self-sustaining language communities. There is no common language the Church can use to express itself to an unbelieving world. Postmodern theology rejects the idea that Christian discourse can be translated into alien tongues without ceasing to be Christian. But then it seems that Christian discourse is the in-language of an in-group, cut off from a larger commonwealth. But this is to forget that people can learn to speak more than one language without recourse to a third, common tongue.

Finally, we must consider the question of violence, for it is said that despite all its talk about "harmony" and "peace," narrativist theology is itself violent in thinking the Christian story a master narrative that positions all other stories. It is the violence of having the last word. In response, it may be noted that the Christian story is always provisional because not yet ended. It is performed in the hope that the one of whom it speaks will return again to say it. The last word is yet to be said; and when it is, the Church will find herself positioned, out-narrated. Thus the narrativist might make the plea that the Christian story resists mastery by being the prayerful tale of one who came in the form of a servant and who will return as a friend. Nevertheless, the resistance of mastery often requires the resistance of some Christians to others — and here there lurks the suspicion that Christian faith is finally only a ruse of Nietzsche's "will to power." This, perhaps, is what must always remain undecidable in Christianity, or in any other faith.

Newman's Radical Orthodoxy

In the October 1870 issue of *The Edinburgh Review*, John Tulloch concluded his anonymous review of John Henry Newman's *Essay in Aid of a Grammar of Assent*, by noting that while it was the product of Romanism's perhaps "finest mind," it was yet a work of "intellectual havoc and the audacious yet hopeless dogmatism which it teaches."[49] Newman, his mind "intensely dogmatic and authoritative," abandons not only reason but argument in "reference to his faith," and refuses to "look around."[50] He attempts to render faith secure from criticism simply by refusing its claims. Tulloch, of course, was not the first to say this of Newman's thought, nor the last. But what he found unacceptable in Newman is precisely that which opens Newman to a postmodernist reading, as a sort of narrativist theologian.

It is precisely at the point where Newman rejects liberalism, that he accepts, or opens the way to accepting, the radically textual, mediated nature of the world. For Newman, what always comes first is faith, an imagining of how the world is, a symbolic view or master narrative, within which reason operates. The liberal quaintly

---

[49] [John Tulloch], "Dr. Newman's *Grammar of Assent*," *The Edinburgh Review* 132 (October 1870) 382-414, 414.

[50] Tulloch, "Dr. Newman's *Grammar of Assent*," 391-392.

supposes that the world can be viewed impartially, without preju-
dice. We open our eyes and take a good look, and having established the facts we then go on to infer a view of the world from
which we may eventually conclude that there is a God, probably.
"First comes knowledge, then a view, then reasoning, and then
belief."[51] But this, for Newman, is to get matters back to front, and
even if it gets us somewhere, it will never get us to that belief which
is of the heart; a passion that changes lives. This is what Newman
meant by the dogmatic principle. Faith is held as dogma, not against
reason, but as that within which reason operates, as that embodied
complex of doctrinally ruled stories, symbols and rites, which gives
rise to faith as its expression. This, after all, is the labour of Newman's *Essay in Aid of a Grammar of Assent*, to offer a thick,
detailed description of how it is that in the manifold messiness of
human life, the religious imagining of the world can take hold of
mind and body, transforming us into the family of Jesus Christ.

> The heart is commonly reached, not through the reason, but through
> the imagination, by means of direct impressions, by the testimony of
> facts and events, by history, by description. Persons influence us, voices
> melt us, looks subdue us, deeds inflame us. Many a man will live and
> die upon a dogma: no man will be a martyr for a conclusion. ... Life
> is for action. If we insist on proofs for every thing, we shall never come
> to action: to act you must assume, and that assumption is faith.[52]

Newman is not a fideist, if by fideism we suppose a faith that cannot give a reasonable account of itself, that cannot show how it is
impelled by the mystery of the world. Rather Newman is a non-
foundationalist, for whom those beliefs that are most basic to a person's imagining of the world can only be held as assumptions, and
that there is no one for whom this is not the case. The assumption

---

[51] *GA*, 65.
[52] *Ibid.*, 66-67.

of first beliefs — the inhabiting of the fundamental stories by which
we live — is not irrational, but that which permits reason in the first
place, since reason can only operate within an always prior assumption. The assumption of faith gives us a meaningful world in which
we can live and reason. And it is this non-foundationalist stance,
this recognition that we must always begin in the middle, that postmodernism has sought to generalise.

Unlike modernism, which fondly imagined an assumption-free
zone from which to view the world, postmodern thought ventures that
all points of view must first assume what they can see. Admittedly,
postmodern culture secretly retains a modernist moment, that allows
it to resist relativizing absolutely everything, and most particularly
the laws of consumption, whose religious observance produces an
ever-burgeoning array of consumer beliefs. Postmodern dogmatic theology rejects the modernist assumption of a hegemonic non-theological reason, and, in holding to its own view of the world, it also rejects
the modernist moment of consumer capitalism. Thus, unlike the retail
beliefs of secular postmodernism, which must never be taken too seriously for fear that they will be banned from the market place, postmodern dogmatic theology holds only to itself, to the view that the
world is creation rather than happenstance. For such a theology, the
world is drenched with meanings requiring discernment rather than a
Void that remains silent in the face of our entreaties. This means that
a postmodern theology which imagines a God who has given us the
gift of imagination — as opposed to a postmodern theology for which
God is merely a comforting idol, a play-thing — is a dangerous kind
of theology, which at worst will authorize our violence, and at best
lead us to venture our lives upon impossible dreams. For, as Newman
often reminds us, it is above all in the stories of the Christian martyrs
that we see what it is to "live and die upon a dogma."[53]

---

[53] *Ibid.*, 66.

NEWMAN AND THE PARTICULARITY OF CONSCIENCE

Gerard J. Hughes

1. The Issues

Professor John Finnis, in his discussion of Newman's *Letter to the Duke of Norfolk*,[1] disputes Newman's claim that conscience and infallible Papal teaching cannot conflict. Finnis's criticisms of Newman are several, and some of them form the interpretative background to the others. Thus, Newman is said to make the mistake of "bundling together" such quite different matters as positive law, Church discipline, ritual, and moral teaching.[2] The danger in this approach, in Finnis's view, is partly that moral teaching is downgraded in its importance, and, more fundamentally, its claim to truth is obscured by being lumped together with positive laws; teaching, after all, is quite distinct from lawmaking.[3] Perhaps Finnis also thinks that by associating moral teaching with such changeable regulations, it is easier for Newman to make his case about moral teachings.

Finnis also finds the examples cited by Newman in the section on "Double Allegiance" less than conclusive. Newman wishes to argue that the occasions on which Popes have in fact issued moral

---

[1] John Finnis, "Conscience in the *Letter to the Duke of Norfolk*," *Newman after a Hundred Years*, ed. Alan G. Hill and Ian T. Ker (Oxford: Clarendon, 1990) 401-418.

[2] *Ibid.*, 404.

[3] *Ibid.*, 406.

condemnation are so rare and deal with such unusual cases as hardly to be a burden on any ordinary Catholic. The examples in which there might be a case for disobeying a papal command are so hypothetical as to be in practice irrelevant. Finnis offers alternative examples which are more troublesome, and suggests that even Newman's cases might not seem as far fetched nowadays as perhaps they seemed in the calmer moral climate of the 1870's. I will come back to this aspect of Finnis's argument later.

In general, though, according to Finnis, Newman smoothes over potential conflicts and difficulties, in order to suggest that Gladstone has greatly exaggerated the impact of the Vatican definition. Finnis's own reply would have been far less comforting, much more uncompromising: "The primary true reply to that accusation is that the Church's irreformable teachings are not a burden but an enlightenment."[4]

But Finnis's central criticism of Newman is that the key argument, developed by Newman in the section of the letter on "Divided Allegiance," elaborated in the section on "Conscience," and repeated in connection with "The Vatican Definition" simply does not work. Newman's argument runs as follows:

> The judgements of conscience concern particular actions.
> Infallible teaching is embodied in general propositions, or in the rare condemnations of particular and given errors.
> Hence, "conscience cannot come into direct collision with the Church's or the Pope's infallibility."

Finnis maintains that both premises are false. Moreover, though he does not say so quite in so many words, he would hold that even were the premises true the conclusion would not follow. I shall claim that Finnis systematically misinterprets Newman; and that the position Newman in fact adopts, though perhaps not the only

---

[4] *Ibid.*, 416.

possible position, is certainly a very defensible one. To show this, I shall begin by developing the background against which, I believe, Newman's views have to be read. This will enable me to explain the theory of moral reasoning which Newman presupposes, and hence to show that Newman's first premise escapes Finnis's criticisms. I shall then discuss whether, given the truth of the first premise, and assuming the truth of the second premise, Newman's conclusion would follow. Then I shall offer at least some considerations bearing on the truth of the second premise.

2. Newman's Aristotelian Background

Newman's account of the Illative Sense in his *A Grammar of Assent* endeavours to show that knowledge — justifiable true belief — can be, and indeed routinely is, arrived at by a process of inference which is neither inductive nor deductive. Indeed, this is how our minds work in every subject matter except formal logic and mathematics. Newman quotes what he describes as "the grand words of Aristotle:"

> "We are bound to give heed to the undemonstrated sayings and opinions of the experienced and aged, not less than to demonstrations; because, from their having the eye of experience, they behold the principles of things."
>
> Instead of trusting logical science, we must trust persons, namely, those who by long acquaintance with their subject, have a right to judge.[5]

Significantly enough, the passage from Aristotle comes from the *Nicomachaean Ethics*[6] and concludes the summing up of Aristotle's account of *phronēsis*, practical wisdom. Newman's brief remarks

[5] *GA*, 341-342.
[6] VI, 1143b11-14.

about it are entirely accurate. Aristotle's argument depends upon these key points:

i)   Practical decisions are "ultimate" in the sense that it is impossible to prove that they are correct by appeal to anything more fundamental.

ii) Practical decisions concern the individual action to be done.

iii) Universal principles are built up from experience of individual cases; and hence are the fruit of experience.

iv) Formulating universal principles in the light of experience is again an act of insight, not susceptible of demonstrative proof.

Newman's Illative Sense has a great deal in common with Aristotle's use of *nous* in such contexts. *Nous* is contrasted with *logos*, in that whereas the latter is an ability to reason things out by constructing formal arguments, *nous* is the ability to assess the import of evidence. An Aristotelian *apodeixis* — which Newman translates as "demonstration" — requires a logically valid deduction from premises that are true of necessity. Demonstrations, says Aristotle, are characteristic of the explanations offered by reason when we are dealing with those features of the universe that we are unable to change. Newman quoted precisely this passage from Aristotle because Aristotle makes it clear that the practical wisdom — the *phronēsis* — of the elders and the wise does *not* work by demonstration, but by insight applied to experience. Newman in the *Grammar* goes on to suggest that in order to see what he himself means by the Illative Sense across the whole range of intellectual activity, we can do no better than to look at the workings of moral judgement, where the nature of the Illative Sense, as it is embodied in *phronēsis,* is already commonly acknowledged.[7]

---

[7] *GA*, 353.

What it is to be virtuous, how we are to gain the just and right idea and standard of virtue, how we are to approximate in practice to our own standard, what is right and wrong in a particular case, for the answers in fulness and accuracy to these and similar questions, the philosopher refers us to no code of laws, to no moral treatise, because no science of life, applicable to the case of an individual, has been or can be written. Such is Aristotle's doctrine, and it is undoubtedly true... The authoritative oracle, which is to decide our path, is something more searching and manifold than such jejune generalisations as treatises can give, which are most distinct and clear when we least need them.[8]

In this paragraph, Newman neatly combines the essential Aristotelian points: (i) what it is to be virtuous, and which standards are the true ones, can be derived only from our many judgements in individual cases; (ii) no code of laws or set of moral principles can possibly guarantee their correct application to particular instances; and (iii) our judgement in individual cases is, at least in those who are older and experienced, more demanding and searching than any set of jejune generalities could possibly be.

It seems to me clear that Newman's views of conscience in the *Letter* are exactly the same as those of Aristotle, which he expounds so sympathetically in the *Grammar*. The similarities are worth spelling out in detail.

After outlining the doctrine of conscience that, he avers, is common to Catholics and Protestants, he goes on to contrast it with the specious guidance offered by what amounts to a conspiracy of academics:

The rule and measure of duty is not utility, nor expedience, nor the happiness of the greatest number, nor State convenience, nor fitness, order and the *pulchrum*. Conscience is not a long-sighted selfishness,

---

[8] *Ibid.*, 354.

nor a desire to be consistent with oneself, but a messenger from Him. who, both in nature and in grace, speaks to us behind a veil...
Noble buildings have been reared as fortresses against that spiritual, invisible influence which is too subtle for science and too profound for literature. Chairs in universities have been made the seats of an antagonist tradition.[9]

Newman's targets are unmistakably identified, characteristic phrase by phrase: utilitarians, Hobbesian egoists, Kantians, moral Darwinians, and scientific neo-determinists. In contrast to these academic theoreticians, Newman above all resists any effort to reduce morals to a *system* — whether Utilitarian, or Kantian, egoist or any other — in which some purely calculative or logical process would replace judgement in his Aristotelian sense. Secondly, he rejects any attempt to explain away the personal and moral authority of our conscientious judgments by invoking determinist, or Darwinian, or anthropological theories. Conscience cannot be replaced by psychological theory, nor be accounted for within the confines of a theoretical moral system. It is too subtle for science, and too profound for literature — even the literature of moral philosophy and theology.

In the *Grammar,* Newman quotes Aristotle in support of the view that ethics is not a science, and it is consequently a mistake, the mark of a lack of education, to seek in ethics that precision which one might look for in the physical sciences. Here is his citation and his comment:

> "A well educated man will expect exactness in every class of subject, according as the nature of the thing admits; for it is as much a mistake to put up with a mathematician using probabilities, and to require demonstration of an orator... And so again it would appear that a boy may be a mathematician, but not a philosopher, or learned in physics,

---

[9] *Diff.*, 248-249.

and for this reason, — because the one study deals with abstractions, while the other studies gain their principles from experience."[10] ... These words of a heathen philosopher, laying down broad principles about all knowledge, express a general rule, which in Scripture is applied authoritatively to the case of revealed knowledge in particular.[11]

The "undoubtedly true" Aristotelian doctrine that no "science of life has been or can be written" is a consequence of the fact that exact moral principles to cover all particular instances without further need for judgement are simply not to be had. To hanker after them is the mark of a lack of education. So in the *Letter* the manuals of moral theology, even though "drawn up by theologians of authority and experience," are "little more than reflexions and memoranda of our moral sense."[12] As he has already pointed out, it is always useful to listen to the older and more experienced, since they have (it is assumed) learnt from their experience. But even the wisdom of the wise distilled in the manuals of casuistry are of necessity inexact. Hence, says Newman,

> I should decide according to *the particular case, which is beyond all rule, and must be decided on its own merits.* I should look to see what theologians could do for me, what the Bishops and clergy around me, what my confessor; what friends whom I revered: and if, after all, I could not take their view of the matter, then I must rule myself by my own judgement and my own conscience.[13]

That the particular case is beyond all rule is a corollary of his Aristotelian approach to moral decision-making. How, then, does that Aristotelian person of practical wisdom make a decision? It must

---

[10] The citations are from *NE*, 1094b23-28, and 1142a11-20.
[11] *GA*, 414-415.
[12] *Diff.*, 242, 243.
[13] *Ibid.*, 243-244. Italics mine.

first be assumed, as Newman is at great pains in the *Letter* to point out, that the person is emotionally balanced — has the moral virtues formed by a proper training in childhood. Newman certainly does not hold that conscience by deciding makes something true. Such a position is in itself incoherent. In any case, it is obvious that a person's ability to discover the truth about what has to be done in a particular case can be as yet imperfectly developed (as in the case of the young who are as yet incompletely trained) or corrupted (in the case of those whose unbalanced emotions or desires cloud their judgement). Newman is speaking in the *Letter* and in the *Grammar* of people who possess both Aristotelian natural *phronēsis* and the Christian grace of prudence.[14] He is not using "conscience" in its debased and vulgar sense.

Well, then, the person of true Christian prudence already has, built up from past experience, a large number of moral generalisations to hand. They know in general terms what kindness is, and truthfulness, and courage, and honesty, and that stealing is wrong, as are lying and adultery. They have a highly developed conceptual apparatus in terms of which they can read any situation with which they are confronted. But there are two, or perhaps three, different ways in which this knowledge will fail to produce an automatic answer to the question how they should act in this instance. They might realise that they need to be kind, but not be clear exactly what kindness requires them to say or do right now. How does one break a piece of devastatingly bad news to someone? Again, they might realise that both kindness and truthfulness are relevant in this instance, but not be sure which of them is more important. And perhaps there is also a third possibility, which is

---

[14] Quite whether these two need to be distinguished as Newman does, following the medieval tradition, is a separate question that need not be dealt with here.

that they may not be clear which of the virtues, or moral rules, is even relevant to this instance.

Take Kant's well-known example about the innocent man being pursued by a gang of bandits, who ask you which way he went. There are three things which someone in principle might have to consider: how to sound completely convincing to the gang while giving them misleading information; whether to say that in this case saving an innocent life is more important than truth-telling: or deciding that truth-telling simply should not be an issue at all in this case. Aristotle, and Newman, both deny that one's previous grasp of all these notions and principles will automatically suffice to make a decision. And even in situations where the right decision is obvious, one still has to *see* that fact for oneself: the rules do not tell you that. Moreover, one's notions of truthfulness, for instance, might well be refined in the light of this decision — the particular case alters the interpretation of the rule, rather than the other way round.

Suppose, then, one were to ask whether saying "He went that way" in this instance contravened the principle about not lying. Newman, and I think, Aristotle, would say that to put the question that way misrepresents the relationship between principles and individual cases. Either, because of one's wide experience, one already understands the principle in such a way that one's judgement in this case requires no modification in that understanding; or one's judgement in this case amounts to a refinement in the way in which the principle is to be understood. In either case, the true conscientious judgement cannot contradict a true general moral principle, because in judging of the particular case, particular judgement and general principle are harmonised.

This explains Newman's "distinct" reply to Gladstone's difficulty:

> Conscience is not a judgement upon any speculative truth, any abstract doctrine, but bears immediately on conduct, on something to be done or not done... Next I observe that, conscience being a

practical dictate, a collision is possible between it and the Pope's authority only when the Pope legislates, or gives particular orders, and the like. But a Pope is not infallible in his laws, nor in his commands, nor in his acts of state, nor in his administration, nor in his public policy.[15]

I shall return later to the question whether Newman is correct in his view of the restrictions upon Papal infallibility in morals. For the moment my point is that, given that restriction, he has an excellent reason for supposing, on his own Aristotelian grounds, that papal infallibility and the judgements of conscience cannot conflict with one another. Universal moral principles are inexact generalisations from previous experience; and the judgements of conscience are judgements about this instance, which may or may not lead one to a refined understanding of one's general moral principles and the requirements of the moral virtues, but are in any event epistemologically prior to that understanding.

3. Finnis's Criticisms of this Argument

Finnis begins his principal criticism like this:

> Newman's discourse at this point has shifted, without warning, from the "habitual" to the "actual" conscience. There can be no objection to that: both are legitimate senses of "conscience" and there is no incompatibility between them. But his argument here forgets that the actual conscience, being a rational (even if mistaken) judgement about a particular opinion, is an *application* of rational (even if mistaken) norms and principles of judgement — at the highest level, the principles understood and affirmed in the habitual conscience.[16]

It is my contention that this criticism wholly misunderstands Newman's theory of moral judgement. It interprets Newman

---

[15] *Ibid.*, 256.
[16] Finnis, "Conscience in the *Letter to the Duke of Norfolk*," 413.

against a scholastic background, and indeed against the particular version of that background which Finnis himself accepts, and then proceeds to accuse Newman of carelessly making moves which would be confusing within that system. In fact, though, Newman *never* speaks, either in the *Letter* or in the *Grammar,* of the "habitual" conscience as Finnis understands that term. Finnis draws the distinction as follows:

> But Christian tradition has from the outset used the term "conscience" (*suneidèsis, conscientia*) to refer to our grasp of natural and divine law in all its universality and immutability, *as well as* to our grasp of a particular option's rightness, wrongness, or eligibility here and now.[17]

Finnis is right, "conscience" has been used in both these ways, though whether "from the outset" is open to dispute. Scholarly opinion still differs on just what Aquinas would have said about our knowledge of the primary and secondary principles of the natural law.

Two recent commentators on Aquinas arrive at notably different conclusions: for the maximalist interpretation Denis Bradley maintains that Aquinas's doctrine of *synderesis* restructures the very foundations of Aristotelian moral reasoning. It consists in an infallible insight into universal, exceptionless, positive moral principles.[18] Daniel Westberg, on the other hand, maintains that Thomas's

---

[17] *Ibid.*, 410.

[18] Denis Bradley, *Aquinas on the Twofold Human Good* (Washington, DC: Catholic University of America Press, 1997) 255-256. A typical text to illustrate this approach might be *In II Sent.* d. 24, q2, a4: "Lex naturalis nominat universalia principia juris; synderesis vero nominat habitum eorum, seu potentia cum habitu; conscientia vero nominat applicationem quamdam legis naturalis ad aliquid faciendum per modum conclusionis cujusdam" (Notice that here *conscientia* is what Finnis terms the "actual" conscience). In general, the argument is that such principles express our fundamental natural inclinations. As Bradley himself emphasises, "we only actually cognize the *per se nota* practical principles by first knowing and willing the determinate goods that correspond to our natural

discussion "reveals something important about the content of *syn-deresis*: though it is described as the *habitus* of the general princi-ples of natural law, the content of the principles would seem in the example above to be very restricted."[19] I incline to think that West-berg's view is closer to the truth. In any event, it is not disputed that in Aquinas's view any more specific moral rules will be both less likely to be true in all cases, and less easy to be sure of.[20] So even in Aquinas, the role of habitual conscience is somewhat nar-rower than Finnis would suggest, or than Finnis himself would wish to argue for on his own account.

But it is surely plain that there is nothing of any of this in Newman, and that Finnis's assumption that there is has no textual basis at all. Discussions which seem to Finnis clearly to be dis-cussions of habitual conscience[21] are in fact nothing more than gen-eral remarks about our ability to discover truths about morality according to God's will. The "first principles" which Newman speaks of[22] are not Thomas's *prima principia legis naturalis;* rather they are the universal sense of right and wrong, the consciousness of transgression, the pangs of guilt, and the dread of retribution. Newman contrasts this immediate sense of right and wrong, which he calls conscience, with the abstract theories proposed by

---

inclinations," *Ibid.*, 301-302 So even on the strong view of "first principles," a correct grasp of particular instances comes first.

    [19] Daniel Westberg, *Right Practical Reason* (Oxford: Clarendon Press, 1994) 150. Another sentence from the same article as the preceding reads as follows: "Synderesis hanc proponit: omne malum est vitandum; ratio superior hanc assumit: adulterium est malum, quia lege Dei prohibitum. Elsewhere, Aquinas offers that one should obey what God has commanded; that one should love one's neighbour as oneself, that one should honour one's parents, that stealing is wrong, and that nobody is to be harmed unjustly."

    [20] I-II, 94, 4.
    [21] *Diff.*, 250-254
    [22] *Ibid.*, 253.

utilitarians and the others we have already mentioned. Ethics for Newman is not, as it was for the academics of his day and is for Finnis, a *system*. Newman simply has no doctrine of "habitual conscience" as this was understood, any more than does Aristotle. He therefore does not shift without warning from speaking of habitual conscience to speaking about actual conscience.

Why should it matter, in Finnis's view, that Newman slides from using "conscience" in one sense to using it in another? Because Finnis places great emphasis on the exceptionless negative principles which have an immediate bearing on every particular instance; and by making this claim, he hopes to show that Newman is mistaken in supposing that the abstract and general principles of ethics (with which infallibility is concerned) cannot conflict with the particular judgements of conscience.

> [Newman's] argument forgets that the actual conscience, being a rational (even if mistaken) judgement about a particular option, is an *application* of rational (even if mistaken) norms and principles of judgement — at the highest level, the principles understood and affirmed in the habitual conscience.[23]

I think Newman might have made two replies to this criticism.

The first would be that while it is true to say that principles (such as that stealing is wrong, or one ought not to harm the innocent) do indeed influence our judgements about particular options, we need to be more careful in spelling out *how* they do so. They give us categories with which we can characterise possible particular options by offering us various different ways in which we might read the particular situation and respond to it. But the primary epistemological judgement is not the moral principle; it concerns the moral features of the particular situation and assesses what a particular action would amount to. Would it be an act of kindness?

---

[23] Finnis, "Conscience in the *Letter to the Duke of Norfolk*," 413.

Would it be telling an untruth, and if so, would that matter? Of course, such particular judgements cannot be made unless one already understands the meaning of such terms as "kindness," "untruth" and so on; and understanding the meaning of those terms involves understanding that kindness is a good thing, and telling an untruth is not. But to the to extent that Newman is following Aristotle, the *accurate* understanding of such terms and principles depends upon, and cannot go beyond, the judgements we have formed about this and that case; it is just as true to say that judgements about a particular case are then "applied" to our grasp of principles as it is to say that unless we have an understanding of principles we cannot make any judgements about particular cases. Newman would therefore say to Finnis that, far from forgetting the relationship between principles and cases, he has a better grasp of it than Finnis does.

His second line of reply might be to ask what Finnis means when he claims that "to these universal negative moral norms there are no true exceptions."[24] One might begin by noting that if "these norms" refer to the principles which are uncontroversially believed by the habitual conscience, then Finnis's examples go well beyond the traditional list. They would, instead, be typical of the kinds of principle which Aquinas might have described as "tertiary," and about which he held that they are both less clearly true, and less likely to be accurate in all cases. I suppose, too, that "true exceptions" are meant to be contrasted with apparent exceptions. Of course, as Aristotle recognised,

> Not every action or passion admits of a mean: the very names of some passions include their badness, such as spite, shamelessness, envy; and among actions, adultery, theft, homicide. All these and other similar things are so called because it is these things themselves

[24] *Ibid.*, 415.

that are bad, and not any excessive or deficient amount of them. One can never do right in performing such actions; one must always be wrong. Goodness and badness in such matters does not depend on which woman one commits adultery with, or when, or how one does it[25] (1107a8-17).

One can make principles true by definition as here: or one can claim that some types of action, just because of their very relationship to human fulfilment, are worth doing, or worth avoiding.[26] But even then, it is still a matter of judgement which particular actions truly are instances of the type of action in question. This is why Newman can bundle together legal, moral, ritual, and disciplinary matters: not because there are no differences between them, but because in each of them the relationship between rules and instances is complex in the ways I have just suggested. So, Newman might well argue, it is not an *automatic* matter to determine whether an instance falls under a rule or not; moral judgement is always required.

4. The Case for Particularity

Newman's Aristotelianism (if I am right about the link) involves several assertions:

i)   Universal moral principles are generalisations from the particular judgements in one's experience

---

[25] 1107a8-17.

[26] It is not clear that Aristotle, or Aquinas for that matter, would sharply have distinguished between these two cases, given their shared belief that we are capable of discovering the essential properties of things, and that our use of terms reflects this knowledge. *Per se nota* principles in Aquinas are truths which correctly express the essences of things; "self-evident" in its modern sense is a misleading translation; and "analytic" would be even more misleading.

ii) Such principles, where they not definitionally true, hold only for the most part, thus contrasting with the first principles of the physical sciences.

iii) The possession of *phronēsis* requires intellectual training, considerable previous experience, and a balanced set of emotional responses to situations.

iv) The virtue of *phronēsis* enables one to make correct judgements about particular actions; these judgements are not demonstrable, and cannot be supported by any truths more fundamental than themselves.

v)   Such judgements involve the assessment that it would be correct to see a proposed action in such and such a way — as a case of kindness, or killing the innocent, or adultery, as the case may be.

In the final section of this paper I would like to offer some reasons for thinking that this view is substantially correct.

The first of these assertions can be understood either as making either an epistemological or a genetic point. The two, obviously, are not wholly unrelated. It might be argued that precisely because our universal moral principles are built up gradually in step with our growing experience, their epistemological status is that of an inductive generalisation. This I believe to be true. But it is, I suppose, possible to separate the genetic from the epistemological point. To take the genetic point first. Of any concept it is true that we have to learn its proper use by an inductive generalisation which enables us to grasp the link between the various instances in which we hear the concept being used. Now very many concepts, perhaps all our empirical concepts, have edges which are to a greater or lesser extent indeterminate. Some of them can be defined, even if it is not always clear which instances satisfy the definition; others cannot even be defined in the strict sense — Wittgenstein gives the example of "game;" perhaps "moral" would be another instance.

This genetic point alone would, I think, be sufficient to justify the thought that the correct application of any concept, and hence of any moral concept, to a particular situation will at least sometimes require judgement. But what of the epistemological point? Is there any reason to suppose that the justification of moral statements must in principle be different from other statements? There are two reasons to suppose that this is the case. The first is that it is not entirely obvious what the *point* of morality is. Different moralities can differ precisely in what they think is important or worth pursuing, and it is at least controversial to maintain, as Aristotle would, that there is a clear account of human nature which will settle the matter. The second is that even if it is agreed that morality exists to promote human fulfilment, it is far from clear that this notion will suffice to justify conclusions about distributive justice, or self-sacrifice for the sake of one's friends or neighbours. In the face of these considerations, it is very difficult to maintain that the basic principles of ethics are intuited with infallible clarity.

To be more accurate, it is difficult to see that they are so grasped *if they are taken to be true without qualification.* But once again there are two good reasons for doubting that they should be so taken. Firstly, as I have already suggested, it will be a matter of judgement which cases fall under any rule. Secondly, it is much more reasonable to suppose that the basic principles in question, while true, are defeasible. One can easily admit that, for instance, telling an untruth is wrong, other things being equal, or that homicide is wrong, other things being equal, or that education, rearing a family, and being kind to people are things worth doing, other things being equal. If the doctrine that we have an immediate and infallible grasp of some moral truths were to be sustained, these would be good candidates for being the truths in question. The exceptionless moral principles which Finnis claims we infallibly grasp are in fact much more complex: "Every warlike act aimed indiscriminately at whole cities is a crime…;" "Every directly induced abortion is morally wrong"[27] would be typical examples, which depend upon highly contentious arguments about the precise force of "indiscriminate" and the extension of "warlike act" (does that include blockade?), and "direct."[28]

The first edition of the *Catechism of the Catholic Church* defined a lie as "to speak or act against the truth in order to lead into error *someone who has the right to know the truth*" (§2483), apparently oblivious of the fact that the clause I have italicised is omitted in the immediately preceding paragraph. The problem here is not with trying to refine one's principles in order to state them ever more accurately. Rather, the claim that some principles are exceptionless is made plausible only by making the principles true by definition, and thereby glossing over the many controversial discussions which have gone into the complex formulation. In so doing, the suggestion is that no further controversial discussion is ever called for. The general point is that one cannot reasonably suppose

[27] Finnis, "Conscience in the *Letter to the Duke of Norfolk*," 415.

[28] In fact, Finnis's examples are very various. Apart from the two I have quoted in the text, he mentions intentional abortion, contraception, euthanasia, baby-making, adultery, re-marriage after divorce, and the area-bombing of enemy cities (Finnis, "Conscience in the *Letter to the Duke of Norfolk*," 405). Of these, adultery has never been commended by any reputable theologian; if Finnis means some action which *he would consider* to be adultery, then, of course, he simply begs the question by using a morally loaded term. Again, it is "intentional" abortion which is mentioned precisely to give the impression that the questionable use of double effect in some difficult cases does not constitute evidence that the general principle is true only other things being equal. Somewhat similar arguments surround the complex discussions surrounding the end of life; is "euthanasia" a term which is in itself morally neutral, or is it like "adultery?" And surely nobody can be against baby-making quite generally? Or does Finnis have in mind some particular *method* of making babies; and if so, on what grounds? It simply will not do to use manipulative terminology or persuasive re-definition instead of reasoned argument.

that complex principles, whose very formulation includes all the key question-begging phrases, could ever be grasped immediately; or that they could, when disambiguated, ever be thought to do more than state what is true other things being equal.

There are good Aristotelian reasons for this position. It seems to me that one key difference between us humans and other animals is our extraordinary flexibility. Perhaps because of our relatively enormous brain size, we are not merely capable of creating new environments (for better and for worse), and of adapting our life-styles to them (with greater or less success). Besides being flexible in those ways, any given individual has a wide range of life-choices in which that person could be fulfilled, each of which expresses a different set of priorities. Whole societies might be structured differently, with different views of justice and family structures and property, and yet contribute equally to individual fulfilment. So, although the structures of human physiology and psychology must place some constraints on the conditions under which we can live fulfilled lives, these constraints need not be very narrow. The consequence of that is that although there will be some very general moral principles which will be true, their precise interpretation and the order of priority between them may vary considerably.

Aristotle and Newman both hope to delimit the judgements which will count as wise by specifying that persons of practical wisdom must have emotional balance and a wide experience of life.[29] This move, did it succeed, would indeed temper what might otherwise seem the dangerously open-ended and uncheckable scope given to *phronēsis*. The person of practical wisdom can *explain* the judgements she made: she can say, for instance, that she just saw that this was a time for unvarnished truth rather

---

[29] *Diff.*, 257-258.

than for superficial encouragement; or, in another situation, that
she had to find some way of being polite and grateful, and the
fact that she did not at all like the expensive present she had just
been given was quite irrelevant. What she cannot do, on Aristotle's view at any rate, is *further justify* looking at the situation
in those terms rather than in some other terms — for instance,
that it would have been better straight out to say that it did not
suit, but could she perhaps get the shop to exchange it. There is
nothing more fundamental than the all-things-considered judgement of the person of practical wisdom, nothing more fundamental in terms of which she could justify making that judgement in the circumstances rather than some other.

But the safety-net constituted by the requirement that the person
be emotionally balanced and of long experience is less reassuring
when one discovers that what counts as emotional balance is spelt
out in terms of those emotional responses which facilitate and reinforce the judgements which that person sees to be correct. In short,
there is a circle between the definitions of sound moral judgement
and emotional balance. A person's judgements will be sound only
if they are balanced: and a balanced person is one whose emotions
are in harmony with his judgement. So the standard criticism lev-
elled at this kind of position can be put in terms of a bankrupt intu-
itionism, or as "situation ethics," or as a mere canonisation of the
conventional wisdom of the day.

Here, I think, is the real crunch of the dispute between an
Aristotelian like Newman and a more conservative moralist like
Finnis. Newman is not troubled by the fact that ethics is not an
exact science: or that the manuals of moral theology offer, as he
puts it, "a variety of opinions with plain directions, when it is that
private Catholics are at liberty to choose for themselves whatever
answer they like best, and when they are bound to follow some one
of them in particular." He may have agreed that some of the posi-

tions taken by the Jesuit probabilists at Louvain in the 17th century were indeed too lax; but their general contention that in difficult cases there are often several probable — in the sense of arguably correct — opinions, which are mutually incompatible, and any one of which a Catholic might legitimately follow, that did not bother him in the least. He has confidence in the broad sweep of the tradition, in the God-given grace of wisdom, in the willingness to seek advice in difficult situations, and, by implication, in our ability to recognise the people whose advice is worth taking seriously. The rigorist will consider that confidence far too optimistic, and will endeavour to construct stronger fences to limit the scope of legitimate moral judgement. He will endeavour to make ethics into an exact science, with solutions *deduced* logically from infallibly grasped premises. Where human argument apparently fails to convince, infallibility is invoked to settle the matter, in practice if not necessarily in theory.[30] This is done either by endeavouring to extend the scope of infallibility by appeal to the "ordinary magisterium," or, where that is not plausible, by requiring respectful obedience to teachings which are not claimed to be infallibly taught at all. Newman's comments are as pertinent to these later views as they were in 1870.

The final chapter of Newman's essay is intent on showing that the scope of infallibility is much more restricted than Gladstone imagines. In particular he argues that, even when a particular state-

---

[30] *Diff.*, 229. It is worth noting that radical liberal reformers like the Utilitarians were also rigorists, and would equally have thought an Aristotelian claim to insight in line with hallowed tradition to be no better than "what in others they would be apt to term caprice." Bentham, who makes this remark, is equally scathing about appealing to theological arguments at this point, on the grounds that the theological texts themselves, as all agree, require interpretation, "and for the guidance of these interpretations, some other standard must be assumed." See Jeremy Bentham, *The Principles of Morals and Lesiglation*, Chapter 1.

ment is infallibly made, it still requires interpretation, and that task might eventually re-open issues which were once believed to be finally closed. Moreover, the final interpretation, as with the dictum that there is no salvation outside the Church, may well be quite different from what was originally taken to be its clear meaning.[31] What I think is the essential point, however, is the claim about interpretation; and the need for the individual to judge when something is being infallibly taught, and what that something precisely is. The same applies to the requirement of respectful obedience. It is for this reason that the attempt to remove or even radically restrict the possibility of individual judgement, as being too much of a loose cannon, is in the end bound to fail. Even a decision to obey has to be a conscientious decision, involving an assessment of the credentials of the authority in general, of the way in which it is being exercised in this particular case, of the precise interpretation of what is being required, and of the intrinsic reasonableness of what is being said. In short, authority is a stimulus to thought and honest assessment; but it is not and cannot be a substitute for conscientious decision-making. That, in the end, is Newman's case, and it seems to me unanswerable.

[31] *Diff.*, 333-336.

"HISTORIA VERITATIS"
ON NEWMAN'S *ESSAY ON THE DEVELOPMENT OF CHRISTIAN DOCTRINE*

Bruno FORTE

Horizon and Challenge: Beyond "Lessing's Ditch"

"Since the above was written, the Author has joined the Catholic Church:"[1] the "Postscript" witnesses to that remarkable correspondence between journey of reflection and moral decision which makes of John Henry Newman's *Essay on the Development of Christian Doctrine* a work of enduring actuality, comparable for intellectual vigour and spiritual authenticity to the *Confessions* of St. Augustine. It is the account — well-documented, passionate, even hurried, because written at the behest of a deep interior sense of urgency, and so also "unfinished" as only certain masterpieces can be[2] — of the history of truth, as this has come to speak itself and render itself explicit in time, entrusting itself to human minds and hearts. It is — at the same time and inseparably — the history of the gradual discovery of the light of truth, to which absolute obedience is owed. The two planes correspond to one another so perfectly as to flow naturally into the choice which marked the life

---

[1] John Henry Newman, "Postscript," *An Essay on the Development of Christian Doctrine* (Notre Dame, IN: University of Notre Dame Press, [6]1989) x. This is a reprint of the revised edition of 1878, with a Foreword by Ian Ker).

[2] Regarding this work, Newman himself affirms (cf. *Apologia pro Vita Sua*, ed. Ian Ker [London: Penguin Books, 1994] 211): "Before I got to the end, I resolved to be received, and the book remains in the state in which it was then, unfinished."

of Newman forever: "When he had got some way in the printing, he recognized in himself a conviction of the truth of the conclusion to which the discussion leads, so clear as to supersede further deliberation."[3] From both points of view — objective and subjective — the theme of the work is, therefore, "historia veritatis," the history of truth.

At first sight, this expression appears paradoxical: if truth is such, it transcends time; how then can it have a history? Truth constitutes the foundation and the destination of history, and the criterion for judging history: how then can it be a mere component of historical development? A truth which is resolved into history would not be other than history itself with all the limitations of history's inevitable contingency. Why concern ourselves then with a "history of the truth?" Why go so far as to make of the development of Christian doctrine, inasmuch as revealed truth, the theme of a work, in which what is at stake is both speculative and practical, both in the order of knowledge and in that of moral decision? The answer to these questions — which are entirely legitimate and necessary — must be found in the ambit of the "modern" question of truth, as this was posed in the age of the Enlightenment. In the name of the absolute claims of enlightened reason the distinction was introduced between "contingent historical truths" (*zufällige Geschichtswahrheiten*) and the universal and necessary "truths of reason" (*Vernunftswahrheiten*). On the basis of this distinction, Christianity, founded on the "essential paradox" of the incarnation of God, appeared deprived of any possible claim to absolute truth, and consequently of any universal destination or capability of creating moral obligation. The idea of an "universale concretum et personale" appeared to modern reason entirely inconceivable: that is why Gotthold Efraim Lessing did not hesitate to speak of the

[3] *Dev.*, xff.

"ditch" constituted by the passing of the centuries, a "ditch" impossible to cross even by one who — as he himself claimed to be — "often and with every effort had tried to jump."[4] Against this all-embracing and suffocating claim of reason the Christian awareness will protest in various ways. Kierkegaard will make his protest in the name of the "singularity of truth," maintaining the thesis that "subjectivity, interiority is truth."[5] According to him, that which exists is not a mere "case" of the universal, nor a pure moment of the process of the eternal Spirit, but an absolutely unique individuality, unrepeatable and irreducible by any all-embracing attempt to take hold of it. Freedom cannot be understood as a necessity which determines itself, but if it exists, it is the possibility of pure newness, the un-deducible coming-to-be of the individual. With regard to freedom, truth is either free appropriation and interiority, which grows deeper by existing in subjectivity, or — simply — it does not exist. Allies in the rejection of the claims of absolute reason, other Christian thinkers will, instead, seek in the objectivity of truth the alternative to the challenge of the moderns. This will be the approach of the Neoscholastics, with their return to the Aristotelian-Thomistic tradition.[6] Finally, there will be some great spirits who will re-affirm the

---

[4] Cf. Gotthold Ephraim Lessing, *Über den Beweis des Geistes in der Kraft* (Brunswick, 1777).

[5] This thesis appears frequently in the anti-Hegelian polemic of *Concluding Unscientific Postscript to Philosophical Fragments* (*Afsluttende uvidenskabelig Efterskrift til de philosophiske Smuler,* 1846). It can be said that this work is "the *opus maximum* of Kierkegaard as a critic of modern thought" (C. Fabro).

[6] This approach is initiated by the Nineteen-Century Neapolitan School with the reviews *La Scienza e la Fede* and *La Civiltà Cattolica* (later transferred to Rome) and by thinkers such as Gaetano Sanseverino and his school (especially Talamo, Prisco, Signoriello, Calvanese, Portanova): cf. Orlando, *Il Tomismo a Napoli nel sec. XIX* (Roma: P.U.L., 1968).

Christian claim to truth not in the name of singularity, nor beginning from an abstract objectivity, but in the name of the conjuga-
tion — without admixture or confusion — of truth and history.
To this group — together with thinkers like Johannes Adam Möhler
and Antonio Rosmini — belongs John Henry Newman.

In this light one can understand the challenge to which Newman
intends to respond: if truth transcends reason and thus may not be
reduced to reason's too narrow and pinched dimensions, the modern ideology — constructed in all its expressions on the possibilities of reason — will not be able to advance any absolute claim to
truth. On the other hand, however, truth cannot be reduced to the
daring of the individual, to the heroic decision of the "knight of
faith," who risks remaining prisoner of his solitude. Neither it is
possible to affirm a presumed self-evidence of the truth, which
would exclude any historical mediation, because truth always and
everywhere needs human language to talk to human beings. Thus,
truth is more than history, but yet cannot speak without history.
Beyond any this-worldly horizon, truth of necessity comes to offer
itself in time, to communicate with human minds and hearts in a
way both appropriate and comprehensible to them. In this light,
history presents itself as the place where truth happens, the mediation of truth's self-offering to human awareness, the space wherein
the human being may take the concrete decision to welcome or
refuse it.

Truth and history thus emerge as inseparable in the context of
human knowing; and this in the double sense that the truth lets
itself be known in history and that the knowledge of truth on the
part of the historical subject is necessarily achieved by means of a
development. The "historia veritatis" thus calls for the definition
of three aspects, which constitute, in fact, as many fundamental
themes of Newman's work on the development of Christian doctrine: the first concerns the clarification of the relationship between

truth and history on the basis of the primacy of truth; the second considers the effective development of the truth in history, a development which may or may not be authentic and for the authenticity of which it will be necessary to define the criteria; the third examines the proper dwelling-place and authoritative guaranteeing of the truth, recognising these in that structured community which, in the uninterrupted continuity of apostolic tradition, is founded on the original event of divine revelation: the Catholic Church.

1. "Securus judicat orbis terrarum": The Power of Truth

In the *Apologia,* Newman describes a moment of enlightenment, which was to prove decisive for the rest of his intellectual search and, indeed, for the rest of his entire existence: "A mere sentence, the words of St. Augustine, struck me with a power which I never had felt from any words before... They were like the 'Tolle, lege, — Tolle, lege', of the child, which converted St. Augustine himself. 'Securus judicat orbis terrarum!' By those great words of the ancient Father, interpreting and summing up the long and varied course of ecclesiastical history, the theory of the Via Media was absolutely pulverized."[7] With the words cited,[8] Augustine had intended to reject the sectarianism of those who, separating themselves from the whole, also forfeit their relationship with the truth that unites. What was it that had so deeply impressed Newman in

[7] *Apo.,* 116. In this regard, cf. Ian Ker, *John Henry Newman: A Biography* (Oxford/New York: Oxford University Press, 1988) 182ff.

[8] These words are to be found in *Contra epistulam Parmeniani,* lib. 3, ca 4, par. 24, (ed. Michael Petschenig, 1908; CSEL 51, 131): "Quapropter securus judicat orbis terrarum bonos non esse, qui se dividunt ab orbe terrarum in quaqumque parte terrarum." Cf. Johannes Artz, "Newmans vier Maximen," *Catholica* 2 (1979) 134-152, particularly 138-143: "Was in der Gesamtheit der Kirche als lebendige Überzeugung existent festgestellt worden ist, kann auch feierlich als verbindlich erklärt werden" (152).

those words? It was the simple yet powerful idea of the unifying power of truth: truth is not to be found in any compromise, in any "Via Media." Truth imposes itself by its own power, and demands absolute attention and obedience, uniting that which is divided in the bond which it itself imposes. Only the one who welcomes and offers faithful service to truth can be united to the whole ("orbis terrarum!"), and in this way be "securus," that is free from worldly preoccupations ("sine curis"), because capable of evaluating the scene of this passing world with the gaze of one who sees that which is penultimate in the light and by the measure of that which is ultimate and eternal.

The conviction that truth is one, and that, by the unifying power of its light, it imposes itself on the one who seeks it beyond the bounds of whatever solipsistic adventure, inspires Newman's entire study on the development of Christian doctrine. He writes: "That there is a truth then; that there is one truth; that religious error is in itself of an immoral nature; that its maintainers, unless involuntarily such, are guilty in maintaining it; that it is to be dreaded; that the search for truth is not the gratification of curiosity; that its attainment has nothing of the excitement of a discovery; that the mind is below truth, not above it, and is bound, not to descant upon it, but to venerate it; that truth and falsehood are set before us for the trial of our hearts; that our choice is an awful giving forth of lots on which salvation or rejection is inscribed... — this is the dogmatical principle, which has strength."[9] In this text there is an impressive emphasis laid on the power of truth and its binding nature, and, at the same, on the summons — expressed in terms reminiscent of Pascal — to the "wager" by which one decides for truth, in time and eternity. The two planes — objective and subjective — are both considered by Newman: the truth is neither pure

[9] *Dev.*, 357.

objectivity, external to the mediation of history, nor is it the fruit of an unbounded subjectivity. Truth is the Transcendent, which communicates itself, by means of language and historic mediation, to the understanding and heart of human persons, demanding their intellectual assent and free moral decision.

It is not difficult to understand how distant this approach is from the subjectivism so dear to the greater part of modern culture, beginning with the Protestant principle of "free enquiry." It is Newman himself who characterises this cultural stance, rejected by him, with an accurate description: "That there is no truth;... that our merit lies in seeking, not in possessing; that it is a duty to follow what seems to us true, without a fear lest it should not be true; that it may be a gain to succeed, and can be no harm to fail; that we may take up and lay down opinions at pleasure; that belief belongs to the mere intellect, not to the heart also; that we may safely trust to ourselves in matters of Faith, and need no other guide, — this is the principle of philosophies and heresies, which is very weakness."[10] The historical element, which truth necessarily uses to communicate with human beings, does not therefore justify any relativism or subjectivism: the acceptance or rejection of truth by the human subject neither adds strength to truth nor deprives it of such. The subjectivist position leaves human beings in their solitude, in a condition of limitless weakness; the power of truth, instead, ransoms them from every form of solipsism, and sets them free in the bond which transcends all and unites all.

History is thus understood as the hermeneutic mediation of truth, and not as the gradual process by which truth constitutes itself. If truth were thus to be resolved entirely into history, the victory would go to relativism, entirely incapable of guaranteeing that history remains open to the surprises of the Transcendent and its

[10] *Dev.*, 357ff.

advent in revelation. Truth "happens" in history; it does not "become" in history. It communicates itself, that is, in events and words, whose capacity to mediate truth is always exceeded by truth itself. The exercise of the historical hermeneutic in the recognition of truth is not, therefore, achieved at the cost of a loss of the onto- logical depth of truth, and consequently of its being imprisoned by ideology and relativism. This means that the enquiry aimed at dis- cerning the truth in its historical self-communication does not in any way presuppose a foregoing of the possibility of a metaphysics. On the contrary, the attention to historical becoming as the con- crete place of the advent of truth, does not exclude, but rather requires, attention to the being of truth itself. Happening in history, truth does not forego its ontological depth; rather, truth simply ren- ders that ontological level — at least partially — accessible, com- municable and meaningful for the human person. The search for the meaning of truth, of truth proposing itself as meaningful and eloquent for the lives of human beings, is not, in short, achieved at the cost of the objectivity of truth; rather, it is a question of truth in itself making itself truth for us, without foregoing its transcen- dence. Truth offers itself to the horizon of meaning, renders itself intelligible and relevant, not by foregoing its power to exceed all intelligibility, but precisely thanks to that power and to the preser- vation of it.

The decisive No to every form of relativism does not signify that the historical element becomes irrelevant to knowing the truth. On the contrary, Newman is entirely aware of the importance, of the limits and of the risks of the historical mediation by which truth offers itself so as to be attained by human beings. In fact, he writes: "A conviction that truth was one; that it was a gift from without, a sacred trust, an inestimable blessing; that it was to be reverenced, guarded, defended, transmitted; that its absence was a grievous want, and its loss an unutterable calamity;... — all this is quite consistent with perplexity or mistake as to what was truth in particular cases, in what way doubtful questions were to be decided, or what were the limits of the Revelation."[11] Precisely when truth in its self-communication offers itself to the mediation of history, it inevitably exposes itself to the ambiguity, complexity and even to the "opinability" of history itself. This is the state of affairs which requires discernment, criteria, an authority to which to refer in order to find direction and confirmation: the "dogmatical principle." The fact, that is, that the truth exists, and communicates itself to human beings through revelation, not excluding historical mediation but rather presupposing it, requires that the trustworthiness of this mediation be evaluated on the basis of trustworthy criteria. In this way, the power of truth can express itself not only in a synchronic sense, uniting minds and hearts in the bond of the obedience it requires, but also in a diachronic sense, through a development which can be authentic or not, and consequently needs to be examined. In this way, too, "securus judicat orbis terrarum"!

2. "Ex umbris et imaginibus in veritatem": The History of Truth

"Ex umbris et imaginibus in veritatem" is the expression inspired by Athanasius[12] which Newman chose for his epitaph, as if recognizing in it the synthesis of his own life and message. It expresses the journey of human knowledge which from the darkness of ignorance and of mere evocation — proper to worldly contingency —

---

[11] *Dev.*, 360.

[12] Cf. *Oratio II contra Arianos*, 81 (PG 26, 319s.) Referring to 1 Cor 1:21 Athanasius contrasts the knowledge of God through created things "per imaginem et umbram" to the "vera Sapientia," revealed in the Incarnation and the death of the Son on the Cross. Cf. Artz, "Newmans vier Maximen," particularly 147-151.

can advance towards the deep reality of the one thing necessary, the truth in its purest ontological reality. This is the interpretation offered, for example, by Ian Ker: "Out of unreality into Reality."[13] Yet the formula may also be seen to indicate the journey to be undertaken within truth itself, from a true even if shadowy and image-bound knowledge, to the face-to-face vision which will be granted in heaven; and, in this second sense, it can evoke the journey that the truth itself makes in the hearts of human beings and in history to render explicit its own riches, only partially present to the awareness of those who first received the gift of revelation. On the subjective plane, this itinerary corresponds to the growth in the knowledge of the faith, which expresses itself in the progress of spiritual wisdom and of theological elaborations. On the objective and community plane, it refers to the development of Christian doctrine within the more general development of the history of the Church.

This last meaning is what constitutes the theme of the work that also marks Newman's entrance into the Catholic Church. He himself describes it thus: "When developments in Christianity are spoken of, it is sometimes supposed that they are deductions and diversions made at random, according to accident or the caprice of individuals; whereas it is because they have been conducted all along on definite and continuous principles that the type of the Religion has remained from first to last unalterable."[14] What Newman rejects in this text (and in the whole work) is both an historicizing conception of the development of Christian doctrine — according to which such development would be due to purely contingent and chance causes —, as well as a subjective conception, which binds the development to the creative decision of

---

[13] Ker, *John Henry Newman*, 745.
[14] *Dev.*, 323ff.

individual personalities. Both cases are based on interpretations, which conceive development as unconnected by an interior law to the truth itself. What, instead, Newman defends — and seeks to demonstrate by very varied historical and theological exemplifications — is a conception of development at the same time objective, organic and rooted in the intrinsic potentialities of revealed truth.

On the basis of this understanding, Newman identifies seven characteristics of authentic development, of which three can be referred to what may be called the "principle of objectivity" — the permanence of the type, the continuity of principles, structural coherence (the first, second and fourth characteristics) —, two to the principle that may be described as that of the development of the intrinsic potentialities, in reference both to the past — conserving action (sixth characteristic) —, as well as to the future — anticipations of the development to come (fifth characteristic) —, two, finally, that may be referred to what can be called the "principle of organicity" — the vital assimilation of the new and the perennial vigour (third and seventh characteristic). "There is no corruption if it (an idea) retains one and the same type, the same principles, the same organization; if its beginnings anticipate its subsequent phases, and its later phenomena protect and subserve its earlier; if it has a power of assimilation and revival, and a vigorous action from first to last."[15] It is no surprise that — in his anti-subjectivist concern, related to the claims of the subject in the cultural and spiritual milieu of the modern era — Newman gives greater attention to the criteria related to the principle of objectivity. Nevertheless, the threefold classification shows that the conception of development presented by him inseparably joins the transcendence and objectivity of the truth to the evolution by which it is perceived through the mediation of history and the organic growth of the ecclesial body,

[15] *Dev.*, 171ff.

rendered fruitful by the limitless sap of the truth which enlightens and saves.

Truth thus has a history: both the history of its gradual self-communication to human beings till the "fullness of time" (cf. Gal 4:4; Eph 1:10), as well as the history of the progressive assimilation of the gift received by the people generated through the obedience of faith. From the meeting between the divine self-communication and the acceptance of faith there is also born a further sense in which we may speak of a history of the truth: that of the very potentialities of the truth, which come to express themselves progressively through the growth of those who receive the truth, and through the variety of circumstances and challenges which demand an ever new drawing-out of enlightenment from the treasury of revelation. Newman describes this structured and complex dynamism thus: "Even after his coming, the Church has been a treasure-house, giving forth things old and new, casting the gold of fresh tributaries into her refiner's fire, or stamping upon her own, as time required it, a deeper impress of her Master's image... Divine teaching has been in fact, what the analogy of nature would lead us to expect, 'at sundry times and in divers manners', various, complex, progressive, and supplemental of itself. We consider the Christian doctrine, when analyzed, to appear, like the human frame, 'fearfully and wonderfully made'; but they [the advocates of other theories] think it some one tenet or certain principles given out at one time in their fulness, without gradual enlargement before Christ's coming or elucidation afterwards... They are ever hunting for a fabulous primitive simplicity; we repose in Catholic fulness."[16] The history of the truth thus becomes inseparable from the place where it dwells and lives in human time: the Church. The movement "ex umbris et imaginibus in veritatem" leads

---

[16] *Dev.*, 382.

naturally to that port in which is to be found the fullness of truth and the development of doctrine achieved in an authentic way.

3. "Nunc dimittis servum tuum... in pace": The "Port of Truth"

"Nunc dimittis servum tuum... in pace": with these words, pronounced by the old Simeon after his eyes had seen the Lord's salvation (cf. Lk 2:29f), Newman concludes his study on the development of Christian doctrine. This is the confession of one who — after much waiting and seeking — recognises the light which enlightens the nations, the glory of God's people. In the most apt way, these words seal the twofold journey: the intellectual journey, with the effort to discern truth in history, and the moral and spiritual journey, with which the author decides to enter the "port of truth," the Catholic Church. "I was not conscious to myself, on my conversion, of any difference of thought or of temper from what I had before. I was not conscious of firmer faith in the fundamental truths of revelation, or of more self-command; I had not more fervour; but it was like coming into port after a rough sea; and my happiness on that score remains to this day without interruption."[17] The intellectual pilgrimage has, in its turn, two parts, the one connected with the other. In the first, Newman demonstrates the full logical coherence of the principle by which the One who has revealed truth in history could not deprive human beings of a living guardian to guarantee that truth's faithful transmission and interpretation. In the second, he proposes to discover that living milieu which receives, transmits and interprets the gift of divine truth ever more profoundly, and he recognises this milieu in the Catholic Church.

[17] *Apo.*, 214.

Revelation offers knowledge of the living God and of his faith-
fulness in love, by virtue of which he will never abandon anyone
who truly desires to know His truth. God has given human beings
the authority of the Church, the necessity of which is demonstrated
by the fact that outside of it truth and history could in no way be
correctly conjoined, and the development of doctrine be achieved
in an authentic manner: "The most obvious answer to the question, why we yield to the authority of the Church in the questions
and developments of faith, is, that some authority there must be if
a revelation is given, and other authority there is none but she.
A revelation is not given, if there be no authority to decide what
it is that is given."[18] The necessity of the authority of the Church
is thus supposed by Newman because of the very fact that there is
a divine revelation in history, with all the developments related
with it: "In proportion to the probability of true developments of
doctrine and practice in the Divine Scheme, so is the probability
also of the appointment in that scheme of an external authority to
decide upon them, thereby separating them from the mass of mere
human speculation, extravagance, corruption, and error, in and out
of which they grow. This is the doctrine of the infallibility of the
Church."[19]

For Newman this conclusion is supported by the insufficiency
of other possible criteria for the recognition of truth in history.
In particular, the criterion of general consensus — invoked by
many as an instrument for the discernment of truth in matters of
faith — is not sufficient even in its best application, that of the so-
called "canon of Vincent of Lérins," to which Newman dedicates
some of the introductory reflections in his *Essay*.[20] According to

[18] *Dev.*, 88ff.
[19] *Dev.*, 78.
[20] Cf. *Dev.*, 9-32.

Vincent's "dictum," revealed and apostolic doctrine is "quod semper, quod ubique, quod ab omnibus" has been believed. But what does this general consensus signify? Who forms part of it? Who is excluded, and why? Newman observes: "It [the rule] cannot at once condemn St. Thomas and St. Bernard, and defend St. Athanasius and St. Gregory Nazianzen."[21] Besides, that which is later made explicit can often not yet be found in the original form itself: thus, Athanasius' creed — which he strenuously defended alone against the majority — could not readily be received applying the canon of Vincent of Lérins, because, although correctly expressing the orthodox faith, it did so in a manner which was innovative in respect of the past.[22] That is why only an organic body, which develops according to coherent and living laws and is regulated by a recognisable principle of unity, can guard and transmit the truth, penetrating it ever more and ever more, while allowing itself to be penetrated by it. This body, willed by God, is the Church. Using Augustine's words, Newman repeats: "No one blots out from heaven the Ordinance of God, no one blots out from earth the Church of God." To separate oneself from the Church is to separate oneself from life itself, from the Christ living in her: "Whoso is separated from the Catholic Church, however laudably he thinks he is living, by this crime alone, that he is separated from Christ's Unity, he shall not have life."[23]

Thus only the existence of the one Church in time and space, according to the plan of God, guarantees the possibility of a development of doctrine which is not its corruption: the application of the seven criteria established for the discernment of authentic

---

[21] *Dev.*, 12.
[22] Cf. *Dev.*, 15.
[23] *Dev.*, 271ff. The quotations from Augustine are taken from *Epistulae* 43 e 141.

development leads Newman to recognise this Church, habitation of the truth which saves, in the Catholic Church. He has no doubt that this recognition would also have been that of the great Fathers in whose school he has been formed: "Did St. Athanasius or St. Ambrose come suddenly to life, it cannot be doubted what communion he would take to be his own. All surely agree that these Fathers, with whatever opinions of their own, whatever protests, if we will, would find themselves more at home with such men as St. Bernard or St. Ignatius Loyola, or with the lonely priest in his lodging, or the holy sisterhood of mercy, or the unlettered crowd before the altar, than with the teachers or with the members of any other creed."[24] Speculative reflection is here joined to historical discernment: the necessity that there be the Church as the dwelling-place of the truth is joined to the effective recognition of this in the Catholic Church, united to its supreme Pastor and to the Bishops with him.

The ontological affirmation of the power of truth, and the hermeneutic affirmation of truth's inseparability from the historic mediation by which it communicates itself, and from the historical developments which this mediation implies, thus flow into the ecclesiological thesis: the history of the truth causes itself to be recognised in a living body, in an indispensable "hermeneutic circle," in a port at which may finally arrive the seeking mind and the deciding heart. This body, this hermeneutic horizon, this port, is the Catholic Church. On the three planes — ontological, hermeneutic and ecclesiological — Newman's study gives cause for thought, but his highest originality lies in having bound the three planes together, in having made of them one speculative and moral itinerary, which marked forever his intellectual seeking and his existential decision. The idea of the development of truth is the unifying

[24] *Dev.*, 98.

key, which allows the theoretical thesis, aimed at affirming the absolute primacy of truth, to bind itself to the hermeneutic thesis, aimed at recognising truth in history, and thus allows the two to flow into the ecclesiological thesis, which recognises in the Catholic Church the living place of the history of the truth: "The idea of development — writes Owen Chadwick — was the most important single idea which Newman contributed to the thought of the Christian Church. This was not because the idea of development did not exist already. But it was a very restricted idea... Newman made it wider and vaguer, and thereby far more fertile in conception, and more useful to anyone who cared about intellectual honesty, or the reconciliation of faith with the evidence of the past which history finds."[25]

Thanks to this key idea, Newman can sing his "Nunc dimittis," even if the way by which he has journeyed to sing it will be the same by which he will have to travel for the rest of his long life, contributing to the development of Christian doctrine in the bosom of the mother Church that he has finally attained. Nor will the law of organic development spare him trials, misunderstandings, resistance, and weariness; yet the light he attained in his work of 1845 will never again leave him. This is why the seal he placed on his study of the development of Christian doctrine may be considered the seal of his whole life and work, which he offers as a gift available to all who in this time of exile desire to open themselves to that encounter with the truth which alone leads to the homeland: "Such were the thoughts concerning the 'Blessed Vision of Peace', of one whose long-continued petition had been that the Most Merciful would not despise the work of His own Hands, nor leave him to himself; — while yet his eyes were dim, and his breast laden, and he could but employ Reason in the things of Faith.

[25] Owen Chadwick, *Newman* (Oxford: Oxford University Press, 1983) 48.

And now, dear Reader, time is short, eternity is long. Put not from
you what you have here found...

Nunc dimittis servum tuum, Domine,
Secundum verbum tuum in pace:
Quia viderunt oculi mei salutare tuum.[26]

[26] *Dev.*, 445.

NEWMAN ON FAITH IN THE TRINITY

Terrence MERRIGAN

1. Introduction

Any reflection on Newman's contributions to theology which
involves an evaluation in the light of contemporary developments
in the field, inevitably exposes certain limitations in his approach
to particular issues. But just as often, it reveals surprising insights
which may have gone long unnoticed and which qualify Newman
as a thinker of more than merely 'historical' interest. As is often
the case with Newman, these insights are not always systematically
developed. They are quite literally 'seminal', that is to say, they are
seeds which Newman had neither time nor opportunity to bring to
fruition.

One such aspect of Newman's thought is his analysis of faith in
the Trinity in the *Grammar of Assent*.[1] Newman's trinitarian and
christological doctrine is generally regarded as one of the least original elements in his oeuvre. As one commentator has observed of
Newman's christology, "he had no desire to be original. He wanted
to be orthodox and to meet the spiritual and intellectual needs of
the day."[2] It certainly is the case that Newman's understanding of

---

[1] All references to Newman's works will make use of the standard abbrevia-
tions contained in the Oxford critical edition of *An Essay In Aid Of A Grammar
Of Assent*, ed. by J. H. Newman and Ian Ker (Oxford: Clarendon, 1985) ix-x.

[2] Roderick Strange, "Newman and the Mystery of Christ," *Newman After a
Hundred Years*, ed. Ian Ker and Alan G. Hill (Oxford: Clarendon, 1990) 327.
See also Roderick Strange, *Newman and the Gospel of Christ* (Oxford: Oxford
University Press, 1981).

the Trinity was largely shaped by his study of the Fathers, and the Alexandrians in particular. The influence of this tradition is evident in his historical writings and in those sermons dedicated to the exposition of Christian doctrine.

In the *Grammar*, however, Newman raises the issue of Trinitarian faith in the context of a discussion which is very close to his heart, and which he pursues by developing his own conceptual apparatus. His concern is to establish that religious faith is, in the first place, an achievement of the imagination and not of the intellect. The conceptual apparatus which he develops is, of course, his celebrated distinction between real and notional apprehension and assent. This means that, while Newman might be treating a classical theme, he does so from a novel point of view and by making use of novel ideas. This is in itself reason enough to look once again at Newman's reflections.

There is, however, a second reason. In two important articles (both of which are included in a recent collection of the author's essays),[3] a prominent English theologian, Colin Gunton, has drawn on Newman's discussion of the Trinity, including the discussion in the *Grammar*, to lay two charges against him. These are, first,

---

[3] Colin Gunton, *Theology Through the Theologians: Selected Essays — 1972-1995* (Edinburgh: T. & T. Clark, 1996) 1-18; 19-33. The first chapter of this book (pp. 1-18) is entitled, "The Nature of Systematic Theology." It was first published as "An English Systematic Theology," *Scottish Journal of Theology* 46 (1993) 479-496. The second essay (pp. 19-33) is entitled "The Nature of Dogmatic Theology: Dogma and Reason in Newman's 'Seventy-third Tract for the Times'." It was originally published as "Newman's Dialectic: Dogma and Reason in the 73rd Tract for the Times," *Newman After a Hundred Years*, ed. A. G. Hill and Ian Ker (Oxford: Oxford University Press, 1990) 309-322. Gunton notes that "revision is chiefly of the closing paragraphs." References will be to the book, *Theology Through the Theologians*. See p. 10 where Gunton speaks of Newman's "refusal to face the question of systematic rationality," and his "tendency to authoritarian dogmatism."

that Newman displays no real interest in developing an integrated or, in Gunton's words, "systematic" understanding of Christian doctrine, and, secondly, that Newman's ultimate justification for the acceptance of doctrine is a blunt appeal to the authority of the church. To put it in another way, Gunton accuses Newman of defending the view that doctrines, and the doctrine of the Trinity in particular, are to be believed (1) even though they are incoherent, (2) simply because the Church teaches them. The upshot of this, according to Gunton, is that Newman "shows signs of lurching into the... error of a complete divorce of dogma from life."[4]

In what follows, I shall attempt both to illuminate Newman's reflections on the Trinity, and to address Gunton's charges. To do this effectively, however, it is necessary to begin with a more general reflection on Newman's understanding of the relationship between faith understood as a personal encounter with God, and the systematic reflection on that encounter which comes to expression in the church's theological and doctrinal tradition.[5]

2. Newman on the Relationship Between Faith and Systematic Reflection

Newman locates the discussion of the Trinity in the fifth and final chapter of Part I of the *Grammar*. He once explained to a confrere that Part I was intended to 'show' that one "can believe what [one] cannot understand."[6] As is well known, Newman attempted to substantiate this assertion by means of his celebrated distinction

---

[4] Gunton, *Theology Through the Theologians*, 27.

[5] See *GA*, 140, where Newman states that "the "notional is the general and systematic."

[6] C. S. Dessain, "Cardinal Newman on the Theory and Practice of Knowledge: The Purpose of the Grammar of Assent," *Downside Review* (1975) 2-3. This description of the purpose of the *Grammar* was recorded by Edward Caswall of

between real and notional apprehension and assent. This distinction is basic to his approach to the Trinity. It is therefore necessary to say a few words about it.

1. *Real Apprehension and Assent*

Newman's concern in making a distinction between 'real' and 'notional' was to illuminate the way in which people relate to a religion's truth-claims or doctrines. *Real apprehension* occurs when religious doctrines are 'regarded'[7] as referring to 'some-thing' which can be experienced.[8] *Real assent* is the recognition that what the doctrine says is true, *in the sense* that it resonates with some aspect of our actual experience of life.[9] Real apprehension and assent are the fruit of the imagination, though assent, as the recognition of the

the Oratory on the basis of his recollection of a conversation with Newman about the book. See also C. S. Dessain, *John Henry Newman* (Oxford: Oxford University Press, 1980) 148. See *GA*, 89-90, where Newman uses 'belief' and 'real assent' as synonyms.

[7] 'Regard' here is to be understood in the sense given it by Newman in a paper written about 1860 (*TP*, 1: 63), namely, as "the active contemplation, by the mind, of those phenomena which come before it, with the attendant capacities to remember them when they are absent, to recognize them when they come again, to observe the order in which they come, to form them into separate wholes, and to trace that wholeness to a unity beyond themselves or external to itself and to give names to those assumed entities."

[8] As Henry Habberly Price pointed out, Newman used the word "real" in its etymological sense, as derived from the Latin "res" (thing) — a usage that would have been immediately understood by his nineteenth-century audience in view of their classical education. By "real," then, Newman "means something like 'thingish'," and "real apprehension" is quite simply the mind attending to one, concrete thing. See Henry H. Price, *Belief* (London: George Allen & Unwin, 1960) 317.

[9] *GA*, 13, 14, 16; see especially pp. 130-131 where Newman attempts to clarify the way in which the individual propositions which go to make up the dogma of the Trinity can be the object of 'real assent'. There he writes that these propositions concern "what is some degree a matter of experience."

truth of a doctrinal claim, "is in itself an intellectual act." However, as Newman observes, it is an intellectual act, whose object "is presented to it by the imagination."[10] Newman drew on both the Romantic and the empiricist traditions to develop an understanding of the imagination as a 'faculty' which allows us to bring home to ourselves the objects of experience.[11] Newman ascribes a dual function to the imagination. In the first place, the imagination is a *synthetic* power that is able to construct, out of the data of experience, an 'image' of the object of experience. This 'image' need not be a 'visual' image.[12] In the second place, the imagination is an *evocative* power that is able to arouse in the subject the feelings and affections associated with the object of experience. As such it is able to inspire the subject to action. In Newman's words, "though real assent is not intrinsically operative, it accidentally and indirectly affects practice," since it "has the means... of stimulating those powers of the mind from which action proceeds."[13]

[10] See *GA*, 89 where Newman observes that real assent "is in itself an intellectual act, of which the object is presented to it by the imagination."

[11] I have discussed Newman's understanding of the imagination at length in *Clear Heads and Holy Hearts*, 48-81, and in "The Image of the Word: John Henry Newman and John Hick on the Place of Christ in Christianity," *Newman and the Word*, ed. Terrence Merrigan and Ian T. Ker; Louvain Theological and Pastoral Monographs, 27 (Leuven/Grand Rapids, MI: Peeters/W.B. Eerdmans, 2000) 1-47.

[12] As David Pailin points out, by images Newman "does not mean a clearly defined visual representation but an awareness of the reality of the object." What Newman is attempting to express, by his image terminology, is a vivid 'realization' of a particular object, a realization so intense that the object becomes a fact in the imagination. See David Pailin, *The Way to Faith: An Examination of Newman's "Grammar of Assent" as a Response to the Search for Certainty* (London: Epworth, 1969) 122; Ian Ker, Introduction to *An Essay In Aid Of A Grammar Of Assent*, by John Henry Newman (Oxford: Clarendon, 1985) lx-lxi, lxi n. 7, xli. For Newman's terminology, see, for example, John Henry Newman, *An Essay in Aid of a Grammar of Assent* (London: Longmans, Green, & Co., 1913) 103, 23-25.

[13] *GA*, p. 89.

Of course, the description of the imagination as both a synthetic and an evocative power is not meant to suggest that there are two imaginative 'faculties.'[14] There is one imaginative "power," as it were, which grasps its object as a concrete fact.[15] Indeed, Newman continually equated the 'imaginative' with the 'real'.[16] Hence, in Newman's works, imaginative or real apprehension means a vivid realization of a particular object or thing, a realization so intense that the object assumes, as it were, the dimensions of reality.[17]

[14] To speak of the imagination and other 'faculties', is not necessarily to advocate what Hick describes as a "discarded faculty psychology." See John Hick, *Faith and Knowledge*, 2d ed. (Ithaca, NY: Cornell University Press, 1966) 76. In the final analysis, however, as Mary Warnock points out in her study, *Imagination*, "it is very hard to find a substitute for the vocabulary of faculty psychology." She is perhaps correct when she maintains that "in fact... such vocabulary is steadily becoming more innocuous as we more and more clearly recognize it as metaphorical" (See Mary Warnock, *Imagination* [London: Faber & Faber, 1976] 196. As the notes preparatory to the *Grammar* indicate, Newman used the terms 'faculty' and 'power' interchangeably as early as 1868. Writing in 1885, he observed that: "A faculty... is the exercise of a power of the mind itself, and that *pro re nata*; and, when the mind ceases to use it, we may almost say that it is nowhere. Of course, for convenience, we speak of the mind as possessing faculties instead of saying that it acts in a certain way and on a definite subject-matter; but we must not turn a figure of speech into a fact." See H. M. de Achaval and J. D. Holmes (eds.), *The Theological Papers of John Henry Newman on Faith and Certainty* (Oxford: Clarendon, 1976) 155, 135. Note the title of these reflections (p. 154): "On the Mind's Faculties existing, not 're', but 'ratione', and therefore only abstract names for its operations."

[15] J. H. Walgrave, *Newman the Theologian* (London: Geoffrey Chapman, 1960) 110.

[16] See Merrigan, *Clear Heads and Holy Hearts*, 41-47, 57-62. See note 8.

[17] Newman was well aware that what was 'real' for the imagination need not have a counterpart in reality. Hence, he could write as follows: "The fact of the distinctness of the images... is no warrant for the existence of the objects which those images represent." See *Grammar*, 80-81, 88. In the case of Christianity, Newman insisted that the imagination of the individual believer must be subject to the communal imagination of the Church. On this issue, see Merrigan, *Clear Heads and Holy Hearts*, 229-254.

The specifically *religious imagination* is the place where the 'objects' of (religious) consciousness are so vividly 'realized' (and so existentially 'charged') that they are able to command the subject's enduring commitment. In Newman's words, only "a real hold and habitual intuition of the objects of revelation" can inspire the deeds which characterize the life of faith, deeds such as the "sacrifice of wealth, name, or position, faith and hope, self-conquest, communion with the spiritual world," and so on.[18]

According to Newman, the 'objects of revelation' are mediated by means of the living tradition of the religious community, its stories, rituals, and so forth. Immersion in the tradition allows for a deepening of one's existential 'grasp', as it were, of the object mediated.[19] (Conversely, the loss of contact with that tradition inevitably results in a diminishment of one's sense of the reality of the religious object).

2. *Notional Apprehension and Assent*

Notional apprehension occurs when religious doctrines are thought of as referring to generalizations, to 'creations of the mind.'[20] *Notional assent* is the unconditional acceptance of the truth of such generalizations. That is to say, notional assent is the conviction that the results of the reasoning process are sound.[21]

Notional apprehension and assent are the achievement of the intellect. They are the fruit of the mind's instinctive drive to provide a comprehensive and coherent account of experience. The tool,

---

[18] Newman, *Grammar of Assent*, 238.

[19] Merrigan, *Clear Heads and Holy Hearts*, 229-254; see especially John Coulson, *Newman and the Common Tradition: A Study in the Language of Church and Society* (Oxford: Clarendon, 1970) 67-69.

[20] Dr. Zeno, *John Henry Newman: Our Way to Certitude* (Leiden: E.J. Brill, 1957) 122. See also 41-45.

[21] *GA*, 52, 73, 128.

which the mind employs in its quest for comprehensiveness, is its capacity for abstraction. As Newman expresses it, the mind treats the "manifold phenomena" presented to it in their relations to one another. "Instinctively," "spontaneously," it compares them, "criticizing, referring to a standard, collecting, analysing... grouping and discriminating, measuring and sounding, framing cross classes and cross divisions." And, by means of this, the mind ascends to a new category of knowledge — "rising from particulars to generals, that is, from images to notions."[22] Notions are inevitably partial and inadequate representations of reality. Newman observes that they "are never simply commensurate with the things themselves; they are aspects of them, more or less exact and sometimes a mistake *ab initio*." At a certain point, "the notion and the thing part company."[23]

This being said, however, Newman consistently defended both the legitimacy and indeed the necessity of the quest for that comprehensive "view of things" which notional knowledge makes possible.[24]

Indeed, he claimed that "we are satisfying a direct need of our nature in its very acquisition."[25] Hence, for Newman, knowledge, understood as "the power of viewing many things at once as one whole," is worthy of pursuit for its own sake — "an end sufficient to rest in and pursue." Indeed, the very "perfection or virtue of the intellect" consists in a "comprehensive view of truth in all its

---

[22] *GA*, 30-31.

[23] *GA*, 46-47, 49. Whereas real apprehension is, in Newman's words, "an act of experience," notional apprehension is "an act of pure intellect." The object of real apprehension is something which "excites and stimulates the affections and passions" (*GA*,12) while the object of notional apprehension is an 'abstraction' or a 'generalization' (*GA*, 9).

[24] *Idea*, 45, 96, 75-76, 113; *Dev.*, 33, 55. See also *GA*, 30-31, 34. See Merrigan, *Clear Heads and Holy Hearts*, 109-114.

[25] *Idea*, 104; *US*, 108.

branches," what Newman calls liberal or philosophical knowledge. In the *University Sermons*, Newman expressed this same view by the, at first sight rather peculiar, definition of philosophy as "Reason exercised upon Knowledge."[26] His meaning is clear now in the light of the analysis of real apprehension offered above. Knowledge, here, is that living contact with "facts," with real existent things immediately present to consciousness, which grounds (or at least ought to ground) all discursive thought. Philosophy is the elucidation and analysis "of what is already presented in consciousness."[27] For Newman, then, the ideal of knowledge is a comprehensiveness of view which is able to do justice to the complexity of the real. This is evident in his description of a 'philosophic' mind as a "breadth and spaciousness of thought, in which lines, seemingly parallel, may converge at leisure, and principles, recognized as incommensurable, may be safely antagonistic."[28] As we have pointed out, the quest for this comprehensive view is natural, indeed necessary, and as such, an end in itself. If it is to be crowned with success, however, it must never lose touch with its roots, namely, with that real apprehension which is the first and primary level of human cognitional activity.[29]

---

[26] *US*, 290-291. See *Idea*, 111.

[27] Mary Katherine Tillman, "W. Dilthey and J.H. Newman on Prepredicative Thought," *Human Studies* 8 (1985) 348. See *PN*, 1: 136. See *US*, 290-291: "Philosophy, then, is... the knowledge not merely of things in general, but of things in their relations to one another. It is the power of referring everything to its place in the universal system... It makes every thing lead to ever thing else; it communicates the image of the whole body to every separate member, till the whole becomes in imagination like a spirit, every where pervading and penetrating its component parts, and giving them their one definite meaning."

[28] *Idea*, 460. See also *US*, 292.

[29] *GA*, 34: "Each use of propositions has its own excellence and serviceableness, and each has its own imperfection... However, real apprehension has the precedence, as being the scope and end and the test of notional; and the fuller is

In the domain of religion, notional apprehensions and assents are primarily the stuff of theology, which includes the church's dogmatic formulations. The latter are, so to speak, the fruit of the church's communal intellect.[30] Theology, in Newman's view, is "always" notional, since it is the process whereby doctrinal claims are "apprehended for the purposes of proof, analysis, comparison, and the like intellectual exercises."[31] Newman acknowledges that such "intellectual acts [are]... not necessary for a real apprehension of the things on which they are exercised,"[32] but he also recognizes that, in the domain of religion, too, the quest for comprehensiveness cannot be restrained. Theology, he says, is "at once natural, excellent, and necessary," by which he means that it is inevitable, rigorous and essential for the defence of the Gospel message.[33] Still, what is true of all intellectual activity is no less true of theology, namely, that it ought to be grounded in the experience of the real. In line with this insight, Newman repeatedly insisted that an integral Christian life must be founded on both the real and the notional appropriation of faith's object. While the "theological habit of mind" might be "distinct" from the religious one, Newman's ideal is a polar or tensile unity of both, "religion using theology, and theology using religion."[34] The theologian, to practice his or her art effectively, must, in Newman's polar vision of things, engage in a "theology of the religious imagination," a theology

the mind's hold upon things or what it considers such, the more fertile is it in its aspects of them, and the more practical in its definitions."

[30] Merrigan, *Clear Heads and Holy Hearts*, 250, 258-260.

[31] *GA*, 55, 119.

[32] *GA*, 129. Newman actually makes this claim when discussing "the dogma of the Holy Trinity, as a complex whole, or as a mystery." Note that the 'intellectual acts' under consideration are "comparison, calculation, cataloguing, arranging, [and] classifying."

[33] *GA*, 148.

[34] *GA*, 99.

inspired by both a "real" knowledge of faith's object, and a genuine commitment to its notional elaboration. Newman was convinced that the attitudes and sentiments peculiar to both approaches can coexist "in the same mind and at the same time."[35] As one commentator has observed, what Newman envisages is a "harmony of deeply realized personal intuitions with the most rigorous exigencies of rational criticism,"[36] something which Newman himself described as the union of a 'clear head and a holy heart'.[37]

In what follows, I shall endeavour to demonstrate that this ideal is very much in evidence in Newman's treatment of the Trinity, and that his approach to this doctrine involves neither the divorce of dogma from life, nor the subjection of the intellect to an imperious ecclesiastical authority.

3. Newman on Faith in the Trinity

1. *The Place of the Discussion of the Trinity in the 'Grammar of Assent'*

In the *Grammar*, Newman's analysis of faith in the Trinity is preceded by a reflection on belief in God's unity, and followed by a reflection on belief in the Catholic Church's dogmatic formulations. This arrangement is more than a matter of historical sequence. Newman is clearly of the opinion that each step along the way involves one in an ever greater degree of notional apprehension and assent. So, for example, he remarks that the Church's dogmatic tradition involves propositions which are "so various, [and]

---

[35] *GA*, 11, 35.

[36] C. B. Keogh, *Introduction to the Philosophy of Cardinal Newman* (Ph.D. dissertation, Université Catholique de Louvain — Institut Supérieur de Philosophie, 1950) 93, 90. (Emphasis ours).

[37] See *VM*, 1: 75. See *GA*, 215. For Newman on the devotional 'dryness' born of intellectual labors, see *AW*, 247.

so notional, that but few can know them, and fewer can understand them."[38] In each of the three cases, however, Newman is intent on demonstrating that the notional component, whatever its complexity, is rooted in a basic substratum which is amenable to real apprehension and assent.

2. The Unity of God

In the case of the doctrine of God's unity,[39] this substratum is the image of God disclosed in the experience of conscience. It is beyond the scope of this paper to discuss Newman's analysis in detail. For our purposes, it is sufficient to note that the apprehension of God in the phenomenon of conscience is not the product of a rational analysis of our experience. It is instead an immediate, existential awareness — Newman calls it an instinct or intuition[40] — that we stand before One who is to us as a father, One in whose presence we feel a "tenderness almost tearful on going wrong, and a grateful cheerfulness when we go right."[41] There is no suggestion here of a private revelation or of some sort of mystical encounter with God. The experience of conscience is, in Newman's view, a universal phenomenon, a "mental act" constitutive of our

[38] GA, 146. As Newman explains, believers are able to assent to these doctrines by means of implicit faith, i.e., their faith that what the church teaches is true.

[39] See PS, 6: 348 where Newman explains that 'oneness', when applied to God, means "that God is one in the simplest and strictest sense... one, as being individual." See the whole of pp. 348-349.

[40] GA, 60-63, 103-104. Newman was never satisfied with his attempts to elaborate the proof from conscience. See Apo., 271. His Philosophical Notebook, vol. 2, contains his major attempt to formulate the argument from conscience philosophically. See PN, 2: 31-85. The whole discussion of conscience is vital to the Grammar. See GA, 104-118, 389-391. That Newman was personally convinced of the argument's worth is obvious from OS, 74.

[41] PS, 2: 61.

self-conscious life in the same way, and with the same claim to authenticity as memory, sensation and reasoning. God is present as the source of the phenomenon, and the person, most obviously the child, who has been secured from influences hostile to religion or moral behavior spontaneously apprehends Him in the "feeling of... right and wrong"[42] which accompanies his or her decisions. (Hence, conscience is described as the "voice" of God, or the "echo" of God's voice in us.)[43]

It would seem that, for Newman, the experience of God as "a living Person" — and hence as a particular subject — would seem to constitute the basis for the subsequent inference (i.e., notional apprehension) that He is One (i.e., "a living *Monas*,... 'unus', not 'unum', because of the inseparability of His Nature and Personality").[44] In any case, what the discussion in the *Grammar* — not to mention Newman's lifelong attachment to the argument from conscience — makes clear, is that "the proposition that there is One Personal and Present God" can be held not only "as a theological truth," but also "as a religious fact or reality."[45] It is essential to bear this in mind when Newman moves to the consideration of God's tri-unity.

3. *The Trinity as an Object of Faith*

Within the context of this consideration, Newman enquires whether the doctrine that God "is really Three, while he is absolutely

---

[42] *PN*, 2: 49, 37, 43, 99; *GA*, 105; *PS*, 5: 318. See also *PN*, 2: 31 n. 2, 59-60; *PS*, 7: 199-200. Regarding Newman's two-fold distinction of the phenomena of conscience, see *GA*, 105.

[43] *GA*, 107-112; *SN*, 327. See also *Idea*, 61-67, where Newman provides a lengthy discussion of the theological truths which can be gleaned from the experience of conscience. See Merrigan, *Clear Heads and Holy Hearts*, 138-139.

[44] *GA*, 125.

[45] *GA*, 119.

One,"[46] can be the object of real apprehension and assent. His answer is that it cannot, since the "Holy Trinity in Unity" is a "mystery, which you can describe as a notion, but cannot depict as an imagination."[47] At this point the tremendous import of Newman's distinction between real and notional apprehension and assent makes itself felt. At first sight, it would appear that Newman's carefully crafted conceptual tool fails just when it is most essential, namely, when the central doctrine of Christianity is at stake. After all, within Newman's framework, if the triune God cannot be 'depicted' by the religious imagination, then it cannot be the object of those feelings and affections which are able to inspire religious commitment.

Newman's solution to this apparent impasse is as simple as it is theologically sound. He points out that while the *doctrine* of the Trinity, when "viewed *per modum unius*," or "as one whole,"[48] is beyond our grasp, the component propositions are (individually)

---

[46] *GA*, 125. Newman's way of posing the question of whether the doctrine of the Trinity "can become the object of real apprehension" (126) may confuse the unwary reader, since although he repeatedly insists that the dogma "as a whole" is only susceptible of notional assent (140), he sometimes seems to claim that it is also "addressed to the imagination" and is susceptible of real assent. In fact, Newman never simply refers to the doctrine *as such* as the object of real assent, and where he may appear to do so he in fact always qualifies his remarks. So, for example (p. 126), he writes as follows: "The question before me is whether in any sense it [the doctrine] can become the object of real apprehension, *that is, whether any portion of it* may be considered as addressed to the imagination..." Or again (p. 126): "I ask, then, as concerns the doctrine of the Holy Trinity, *such as I have drawn it out to be*, is it capable of being apprehended otherwise than notionally?" Consider, finally, the following (p. 127): "... Does [the doctrine] admit of being held in the imagination, and being embraced with a real assent? I maintain it does... there being nothing *in the exposition of the dogma*, as I have given it above, which does not address the imagination, as well as the intellect." (The emphases are ours.)

[47] *GA*, 132.

[48] *GA*, 129.

susceptible of real assent and apprehension. These propositions are nine in number:

> 1.There are Three who give testimony in heaven, the Father, the Word or Son, and the Holy Spirit. 2. From the Father is, and ever has been, the Son. 3. From the Father and Son is, and ever has been, the Spirit. 4. The Father is the One Eternal Personal God. 5. The Son is the One Eternal Personal God. 6. The Spirit is the One Eternal Personal God. 7. The Father is not the Son. 8. The Son is not the Holy Ghost. 9. The Holy Ghost is not the Father.

The *Grammar* was by no means the first occasion on which Newman had insisted that the doctrine of the Trinity, taken in its most obvious sense — i.e., as the claim that 'These three are one' — could only possess genuinely religious significance when it was, so to speak, 'dissected'. Remarks to this effect can be found in Newman's attack on rationalism in *Tract 73* (1835), in a sermon on the Trinity dating from before 1842, in his sermon notes, in theological and philosophical jottings composed during the 1850's, and even in an anonymous letter by himself to himself in his capacity as editor of the *Rambler*.[49]

In all of these instances, the gist of Newman's argumentation is the same, namely, that there is nothing in the content of the individual propositions which does not resonate with our actual experience. This is, of course, the essence of the description of real apprehension and assent which we offered at the outset. Clearly, by the time he came to write the *Grammar*, Newman had refined his understanding of these concepts. However, he had been working with the 'raw material' of his distinction from a much earlier date. So, for example, one author has noted that the verb, 'to realize', is very nearly a technical term in Newman's vocabulary.

---

[49] *Ess*, 1: 52; *PS*, 6: 347; *SN*, 158, 339; *TP*, 1: 59, 86; *PN*, 2: 106-107, 178; *LD*, 19: 532-533.

Another has claimed that Newman's literary style was shaped by his acute sense of the concrete real and its inherent complexity. This accounts for Newman's frequent recourse to synonyms and provisional definitions, and his demand that literary form be one with the content it aims to express. All of this reflects Newman's endeavour both to remain faithful to, and adequately express, his own deepest experience.[50]

In the *Grammar*, Newman insists that the terms which go to make up the individual propositions implied in the doctrine "address the imagination, as well as the intellect." None of them are, strictly speaking, "scientific terms," none of them are "peculiar to theology." All "have a popular meaning, and all are used according to that obvious and popular meaning, when introduced into Catholic dogma." Of course, Newman is well aware that these words cannot be applied to God in a univocal fashion. As he observes, "No human words indeed are worthy of the Supreme Being, none are adequate; but we have no other words to use but human, and those in question are among the simplest and most intelligible that are to be found in language."[51] It is precisely their simplicity, their unambiguous correspondence with dimensions of our experience, which make theme so suitable for religion — where religion is understood as the vital and intimate relationship between a human person and a personal God. As Newman remarks in the early stages of the *Grammar*, "religion, as being personal, should be real."[52]

Newman's sensitivity to the need for simplicity in the presentation of the faith, if the imagination is to be activated, was also in

[50] Paul Sobry, *Newman en zijn Idea of a University* (Brussels: Standaard, 1936) 57-59, 64-66.

[51] *GA*, 127.

[52] *GA*, 55.

evidence long before he came to write the *Grammar*.[53] A particularly interesting example of the presence of this theme is to be found in a sermon on the Trinity preached sometime before 1842. There Newman points out that it is characteristic of both the Gospels and the early creeds that they reflect on the nature of God's tri-unity by means of "the plainest and most exact form of speech which human language admits of," namely, "common words used in their common sense." What is most striking, however, is Newman's assertion that the object of any "exposition" of the Trinity (as distinct from an "explanation" of it), is to 'impress' on "our mind *what* it is that the Catholic Church means to assert" (emphasis Newman), thereby "making it a matter of *real faith and apprehension*, and not a mere assemblage of words"[54] (our emphasis).

Newman's conviction that faith is generated (so to speak), first and foremost, by the concrete and the tangible, i.e., by the 'real', is basic to his understanding of revelation. It is precisely this feature of Christianity which constitutes it as the completion and fulfillment of the knowledge of the one God disclosed by the experience of conscience. Historical events now display, the teaching Church bears witness to, the moral order disclosed within; history teaches what had hitherto been garnered only by investigation; the Divine Nature is no longer revealed "in His moral laws, but in His spoken commands;"[55] fear is overcome by the fact of divine forgiveness, realized in Christ's life, death, and resurrection and celebrated in the community of His followers. It is the historical character of Christianity which constitutes both "the evidence of the truth of the revelation" and "the media of its impressiveness."[56]

---

[53] *GA*, 55, 98.
[54] *PS*, 6: 347-348. See also pp. 352-353 where Newman comments on the notion of an "explanation." Compare his use of the word "exposition" in *GA*, 127.
[55] *US*, 30.
[56] *US*, 25, 27, 30-31, 35; *GA*, 429-431.

"Revelation meets us with simple and distinct *facts* and *actions*, not with painful inductions from existing phenomena, not with generalized laws or metaphysical conjectures, but with Jesus and the Resurrection."[57] In Christ, "the revealed doctrine... takes its true shape, and receives an historical reality; and the Almighty is introduced into His own world at a certain time and in a definite way," namely, "in the form and history of man."[58] In him, "God has made history to be doctrine."[59]

For Newman, then, the real roots of the doctrine of the Trinity are to be sought in the history of Jesus and the church's experience of their risen Lord. In line with this conviction, Newman is able to say that "a humble, teachable, simple, believing mind will imbibe the doctrine from Scripture, how it knows not, as we drink in the air without seeing it."[60] As he explains in the *Grammar*,[61] however, what it imbibes (and what the creeds and the church's practice reinforce) is an "image" of each of the three persons of the Trinity in their 'distinctive' relations to the believer.[62] In other words, what the believer comes to know is a Trinity of 'persons', with whom he or she stands in relation. And this knowledge is 'real', which is to say that it is, in some sense, 'experiential'. In Newman's view, the Church has always recognized that this 'first-order discourse' is the most appropriate language for the discussion of the Trinity. So, he observes that the church's dogmatic statements, "even in their most elaborate formularies," do not use the word 'mystery' when referring to the doctrine. There is never any question of glorying in the mystery "for the sake of its

---

[57] *Mix.*, 347; *US*, 27. (Emphasis Newman).
[58] *Mix.*, 347; *PS*, 2: 155, 32, 39; 3: 156. See also *Dev.*, 325.
[59] *PS*, 2: 62, 227; 3: 114-115; *GA*, 57.
[60] *PS*, 6: 339.
[61] *GA*, 136.
[62] *PS*, 6: 357-361.

mysteriousness."[63] This is the case "as regards catechisms and theological treatises," Newman acknowledges, but "these belong to
particular ages and places, and are addressed to the intellect."[64]
The Church, however, "in its dogmatic statements concerning the
Holy Trinity," 'fulfil[ls] the maxim, *Lex orandi, lex credendi*."[65]

As a 'religious' reality, that is to say, as the object of Christian
faith and devotion, the Trinity is not, in the first place, a mystery.
It is the source and goal of the Christian's life. The mystery
emerges only when we seek to order our experience of the triune
God, when we seek to "compare, calculate, catalogue, arrange and
classify."[66] However, the mystery which then makes itself felt is
not a part of the "Divine Verity as such, but in relation to creatures
and to the human intellect."[67] As Newman says elsewhere, mystery
is comparable to a shadow thrown by the light already in our possession.[68] It is not a mere contradiction, and it is certainly not simple ignorance. Rather, if "revelation is a religious doctrine viewed
on its illuminated side, a mystery is the selfsame doctrine viewed
on the side unilluminated. Thus Religious Truth is neither light nor
darkness, but both together."[69]

4. Newman and His Critic

In the light of what has already been said, we are in a position to
understand those remarks of Newman which led to him being so

[63] See *PS*, 6: 327-328 where Newman observes that the feast of the Trinity is
the only mystery which is celebrated simply because it is a mystery. See p. 328:
"... We celebrate the mystery for its own sake, not for our sake."

[64] *GA*, 134-135.

[65] *GA*, 134.

[66] See *GA*, 129.

[67] *GA*, 128.

[68] *PS*, 1: 211; see also pp. 208, 210.

[69] *Ess.*, 1: 41.

roundly condemned by Gunton. In *Tract 73*, composed in 1835, Newman declared that "the Catholic doctrine of the Trinity is a mere juxtaposition of separate truths, which to our minds involves inconsistency, when viewed together; nothing more being attempted by theologians, for nothing more is told us."[70] Gunton seizes on these words and, links them to Newman's remark, in the *Grammar*, that it is not possible to assent to the doctrine of the Trinity, taken as whole. Relying especially on the statement from Tract 73, Gunton accuses Newman of a "refusal to face the question of systematic rationality," such that the Trinity is portrayed as "little more than a dogma to be taught."[71] Newman's aversion to system, Gunton claims, is part and parcel of his "rather dualistic Augustinian theology," according to which "time and eternity tend... to be conceived as utterly distinct realms, the one treated by human reason, the other unknown, but accepted through revelation on faith and by authority."

Newman's Augustinianism comes to expression in both his theological methodology and in his approach to dogma.[72] At the methodological level, it is manifest in his "tendency to see theology and philosophy as externally related, to be held more in parallel than in genuine mutual enrichment."[73] At the dogmatic level, it is evident, above all, in his treatment of the doctrine of the Trinity in the *Grammar*. There, according to Gunton, Newman describes the dogma as "'notional', [as] a revelation to be accepted

---

[70] *Ess.*, 1: 52.

[71] Gunton, *Theology Through the Theologians*, 10. See also pp. 26-27.

[72] Gunton, *Theology Through the Theologians*, 21, 28. See p. 24 where Gunton describes Newman's "dialectic of time and eternity" as "the key to his conception of dogma."

[73] Gunton, *Theology Through the Theologians*, 9. Gunton also speaks of Newman's "tendency to authoritarianism, to see dogma as a given to be defended, rather than a relatively open body of tradition with which to critically engage."

on faith as the eternal truth of God. It is notional as belonging to the eternal world, as, so to speak, coming down directly from heaven, and is therefore not the object of rational exploration." This is the basis for Gunton's charge, already mentioned, that Newman divorces dogma from life. The upshot of all this is that, "it is not possible to assent rationally to the [doctrine as a] whole..., 'because, though we can image the separate propositions, we cannot image them altogether'."[74] In the course of his analysis, Gunton declares that, for Newman, "talk of the oneness of God is one thing, the product of philosophical reflection, while the threeness is a matter of authoritative revelation."[75]

On the basis of our discussion above, it is clear that Gunton's portrayal of Newman's position is manifestly deficient, and on some points quite simply erroneous.

The most blatant error is the assertion that the oneness of God is a matter of philosophy when it is, for Newman, the primal insight generated by the experience of conscience. One might seek to excuse Gunton by noting that he is discussing the problem of relating 'oneness' to the doctrine of God's 'threeness', but it is clear that Newman presumes faith in the unity of God when he launches into his discussion of the Trinity.[76] As we mentioned at the outset, Newman's consciously arranges his discussion in an ascending order — moving from God's unity, to His Trinity, to the additional doctrines developed by the church to preserve the apostolic faith.

---

[74] Gunton, *Theology Through the Theologians*, 29. The reference is to *GA*, 130.

[75] Gunton, *Theology Through the Theologians*, 9.

[76] See *PS*, 6: 349: "Thus we must ever commence in all our teaching concerning the Holy Trinity; we must not begin by saying that there are Three, and then afterwards go onto say that there is One, lest we give false notions of the nature of that One; but we must begin by laying down that great Truth that there is One God in a simple and strict sense, and then go on to speak of Three, which is the way in which the mystery was progressively revealed in Scripture."

As far as that faith is concerned, it is clear that Newman is of the opinion that it could only be conceived in Trinitarian terms. In this regard, he anticipates a trend in much contemporary Trinitarian theology, namely, a growing recognition that the church's movement towards an expressly trinitarian confession was inspired by a concern to do justice to the apostolic experience. That experience, in my view, consisted of three elements, namely, (1) the memory of the Jew, Jesus of Nazareth, (2) the experience of him as the risen Lord, and (3) the experience of his continuing presence through his Spirit. In its concern to do justice to this experience, the church inevitably evolved towards the confession of the trinitarian God. In other words, as Newman indicates, the conviction that God is a trinity of persons did not originate in the minds of theologians. Instead, it originated in the hearts of believers. The experience of God as triune preceded the theological systematization which ultimately issued in the doctrine of God as trinity. And the systematization can best be approached as an attempt to do justice to the experience. To suggest, therefore, that Newman tended to divorce dogma from life, or that he saw the doctrine of the 'threeness' of God "as coming down directly from heaven, and [a]s therefore not the object of rational exploration" is a serious misrepresentation of his position.

This misrepresentation is all the more incomprehensible in the light of Newman's repeated insistence that the real and the notional are related to one another in tensile unity. As we have seen, far from insulating religious claims from critical reflection, Newman describes the notional appropriation of faith, which is characteristic of theology, as "natural, excellent, and necessary." Gunton's failure to grasp the distinction between 'notional' and 'real' is nowhere more evident than in his assertion that Newman holds that "it is *not* possible to assent rationally to the whole doctrine."[77]

---

[77] Gunton, *Theology Through the Theologians*, 29. (Our emphasis).

In fact, as we have seen, Newman's view is that this is the only assent which it is possible to give to the doctrine as a whole! If it were not susceptible of rational — i.e., notional assent — it could not be accepted at all, since Newman's entire argument is that it cannot be the object of imaginative or real assent.[78]

Finally, it is difficult to see any basis at all for Gunton's claim that Newman regards time and eternity as "distinct realms." It is well known that Newman's view of history is thoroughly sacramental, though this is something which Gunton does not address. The same is, however, true of Newman's understanding of revelation, a theme which Gunton explicitly takes up. The dearth of references to Newman's works might go some way to explaining the charge. In any case, it is difficult to reconcile Gunton's claim with the remark quoted above that, in the incarnation, "the Almighty is introduced into His own world at a certain time and in a definite way," namely, "in the form and history of man."[79]

In sum, Gunton's attack on Newman is misplaced and unfounded. Indeed, the portrayal of Newman on offer here is so far removed from his thought and his concerns that one is inclined to wonder if it is not essentially an argument *ad hominem*.

5. Conclusion

In his book, *The Trinity*, Karl Rahner lamented the fact that "despite their orthodox confession of the Trinity, Christians are, in their practical life, almost mere 'monotheists'." That Rahner's lament extended also to theologians is evident from what he said next, namely, that: "We must be willing to admit that, should the

---

[78] This assent can, of course, be an implicit assent.
[79] *Mix.*, 347; *PS*, 2: 155, 32, 39; 3: 156. See also *Dev.*, 325.

doctrine of the Trinity have to be dropped as false, the major part of religious literature could well remain virtually unchanged."[80]

This may well be the case, but if it is so, Newman clearly does not share the blame. And were the doctrine to be dropped as false, then Newman's writings would certainly be greatly reduced.

If Rahner's assessment of the 'monotheistic' character of the faith of most Christians (and Christian theologians) is accurate, then Newman's rather disconcerting claim that it is God's 'three-ness' which enjoys a real assent marks him out, yet again, as a thinker who dared to be different, and who continues to deserve a hearing.

[80] Karl Rahner, *The Trinity* (London: Burns & Oates, 1970) 10-11.

NEWMAN, COUNCILS, AND VATICAN II

Ian KER

In March 1831 Newman was invited to contribute a history of Councils to a new library of theological works. That summer he began work on the project; but by August he had decided that the Eastern Councils would need a volume to themselves. He told one of the editors of the library that what was needed was "a *connected* history of the Councils... not taking them as isolated, but introducing so much of Church History as will illustrate and account for them."[1]

The comment is significant for two reasons. First, it makes the point that Newman was a *historical* theologian who was convinced that theology should not be separated from history. Thus: "What light would be thrown on the Nicene Confession *merely* by explaining it article by article? to understand it, it must be prefaced by a sketch of the rise of the Arian heresy..." This didn't mean that he *identified* the theologian with the so-called historical theologian: he was not envisaging always "combining history and doctrinal discussion," and in this case he was thinking of reserving detailed discussion of specific theological topics for notes in an appendix to the work.[2]

Secondly, the remark anticipates the way in which Newman was to become acutely aware of the interdependence of Councils which

[1] *The Letters and Diaries of John Henry Newman*, ed. Charles Stephen Dessain *et al.* (London: Nelson, 1961-72; Oxford: Clarendon Press, 1973-) ii: 352-353. Hereafter cited as *LD*.

[2] *LD*, ii: 352-353.

were not isolated from each other but could only be properly understood in relation to each other. We shall see how Newman reacted to Vatican I, immediately prophesying not that the definition of papal infallibility would make further Councils redundant but that there would have to be another Council to complete and moderate the First Vatican Council.

At this stage Newman thought that he could complete the projected history by adding a further volume on Western Councils — although the Council of Trent would need a separate volume on its own. Not only was the work turning out rather differently from what he had originally conceived, but he had realized that just as it is impossible to isolate theology from history so too you cannot study church history in separation from theology. It was not possible to write a history of Councils as though it were purely a matter of historical research. Like any historian a church historian will approach their subject from a particular theological point of view. In Newman's case, he was quite honest about the fact that he would be writing his history in the context of his own attitude to the theological liberalism of his time: he would inevitably be "resisting the innovations of the day, and attempting to defend the work of men indefinitely above me (the Primitive Fathers) which is now assailed."[3]

In the end, Newman's first published book, which was completed at the end of July 1832, turned out to be on a much narrower topic than his own revised plan envisaged. Far from being a history of the Eastern Councils, it was not even a history of the Council of Nicaea, which he later admitted only "occupied at most twenty pages."[4] In fact, it was really a history of the Arian heresy which

---

[3] *LD*, iii. 43.

[4] *Apologia pro Vita Sua.* ed. Martin J. Svaglic (Oxford: Clarendon Press, 1967) 35. Hereafter cited as *Apo*.

gave rise to the Council, which of course could not be understood without an understanding of Arianism. However, not only was it too specialized for the intended theological library, but one of the two editors objected that Newman's view of tradition seemed to be more Roman Catholic than Protestant.

The Council that most concerned Newman during his Anglican period, and particularly the Oxford Movement, of course, was the Council of Trent. When he and Richard Hurrell Froude were in Rome in 1833, they called on Nicholas Wiseman, then Rector of the English College. According to Newman's diary for 6 April, they "had a long talk with him;"[5] it was their second visit. What they heard was not encouraging: to their dismay, they discovered that there was no prospect of reunion between Rome and Canterbury without unconditional acceptance of Trent.

When three years later, Newman delivered in Oxford his *Lectures on the Prophetical Office of the Church viewed relatively to Romanism and Popular Protestantism*, published in 1837, he made clear what this ecclesiological *Via Media* involved for the Tractarian reception of Trent. The fundamental distinction he makes between two kinds of Tradition is the most significant part of the book as it insists on the absolute authority of Scripture (as against the Romanists), while at the same time allowing for the importance of Tradition (as against Protestants). He divides Tradition into "Episcopal Tradition," which is derived from the Apostles, and "Prophetical Tradition," which consists of the interpretation of Revelation and which is a "body of Truth, pervading the Church like an atmosphere," and "existing primarily in the bosom of the Church itself, and recorded in such measure as Providence has determined in the writings of eminent men." It is this latter Prophetical Tradition which Newman

---

[5] *LD*, iii: 276.

maintains may be "corrupted in its details," so that the explicit
doctrines which develop out of it "are entitled to very different
degrees of credit." So far, then, as Councils are concerned, "some
Councils speak far more authoritatively than others, though all
which appeal to Tradition may be presumed to have some element of truth in them. And this view, I would take even of the
decrees of Trent. They claim indeed to be Apostolic; and I would
grant so much, that they are the ruins and perversions of Primitive Tradition."[6]

At this stage, then, Newman sees the decrees of Trent as deeply
flawed, although containing elements of the true Apostolic or
"Episcopal Tradition." By 1841 Newman has shifted his position.
In *Tract 90* Newman attempts to rebut the most obvious objection
to the whole Tractarian theory of the *Via Media*: namely, the existence of the very Protestant-sounding 39 Articles to which members of the Church of England had to subscribe. In his effort to
give them a Catholic interpretation, he had to confront Article xxi,
which laid down that General Councils "may err, and sometimes
have erred, in things pertaining to God." According to the Article,
only those doctrines which "are taken out of Holy Scripture" are
authoritative. But according to Newman, while it is true that Councils may err, this is not the case when "it is promised, as a matter
of express supernatural privilege, that they shall *not* err." And this
promise "does exist, in cases when general councils are... gath-
ered *in the Name of Christ,* according to our Lord's promise."
Nothing is said about Trent, but, as Newman knew perfectly well,
the Church of Rome certainly regarded it as just such a Council,
that is, a "Catholic" or "Ecumenical" or "general" Council.

---

[6] *Via Media*, I: 250-252. Hereafter cit. as *VM*. All references to Newman's
works, except where otherwise stated, are to the standard uniform Longmans edition.

What Newman is at pains to emphasise in *Tract 90* is that the Thirty-Nine Articles can hardly be said to be aimed at Trent since that Council had not yet taken place when they were drawn up; rather, they are directed against "the *received doctrine* of that day, and unhappily of this day too, or the doctrine of the *Roman Catholic schools.*" Indeed, Newman is anxious to show that, if anything, the Articles gain "a witness and concurrence from the Council of Trent," which was also concerned to condemn false teachings.[7]

Anyone reading *Tract 90* can see that Newman by now has reached the position of recognizing Trent as an authentic General Council. But to understand how he has reached this position, we need to go back two years to the summer of 1839 when "for the first time a doubt came upon" him "of the tenableness of Anglicanism."[8] Far from being concerned with Tractarian controversies, he wanted to spend the long vacation on purely academic research: he intended returning to his "own line of reading — the early controversies of the Church."[9] This time it was not the fourth century and the Arian problem but the fifth century and the Monophysite heresy. His reading was intended to be preparatory to various scholarly editing projects But in the course of his studies, he was struck by two "very remarkable" features of the Council of Chalcedon — "the great power of the Pope (as great as he claims now almost), and the marvellous interference of the civil power, as great almost as in our kings."[10] It was obvious that the first aspect argued for Roman Catholicism, whereas the second could provide justification for the erastian nature of Anglicanism. However, as he read on,

---

[7] *VM*, II: 291-292, 295-296, 308.
[8] *Apo.*, 108.
[9] *LD*, vii: 110.
[10] *LD*, vii: 105.

by the end of August he had become "seriously alarmed." He explains in the *Apologia* what had so startled him:

> My stronghold was Antiquity; now here, in the middle of the fifth century, I found, as it seemed to me, Christendom of the sixteenth and the nineteenth centuries reflected. I saw my face in that mirror, and I was a Monophysite. The Church of the *Via Media* was in the position of the Oriental communion, Rome was, where she now is; and the Protestants were the Eutychians.[11]

In other words, the orthodox Christian faith was being upheld by the Pope, whereas the heretics divided into an extreme and a more moderate party. The theological picture of Christendom in the fifth century presented to Newman a very disquieting analogy to that of the nineteenth century, with Rome on the one side, and Canterbury and Geneva respectively on the other.[12]

Newman's first book was meant to be on the early Councils of the Church, even though in fact it confined itself to the heresy that necessitated the Council of Nicaea. The first serious threat to his Anglicanism came from the next but one Council of the Church. As a Roman Catholic theologian, he ended his life as a theologian very largely preoccupied with the First Vatican Council. That event led

[11] *Apo.*, 108.

[12] Stephen Thomas, *Newman and Heresy: The Anglican Years* (Cambridge: Cambridge University Press, 1991) 205, claims that Newman's account here should be viewed in the light of the "rhetorical purpose" of the *Apologia* — "But what particularly provokes suspicion is that Newman does not support this splendid piece of self-dramatisation by any corroboration of letters or memoranda of the time — something he always does in the *Apologia* when he can..." However, this ignores the fact that Newman had every reason at the time to keep quiet about this devastating bombshell for fear of unsettling his Tractarian followers. Yet he was not totally circumspect, writing on 22 September 1839 to his then closest friend Frederic Rogers: "... the whole history of the Monophysites has been a sort of alterative..." (*LD*, vii: 154). The *OED* defines this obscure word as a medicine which produces alteration in the processes of nutrition.

him to reflect not only on that Council but on Councils in general. Much, but not all of this theology of Councils, is to be found in his private letters of the time.

On 26 June 1867 Pope Pius IX announced that a General Council was to be convened. The prospect of the definition of papal infallibility particularly concerned Newman, and not only because of the specific doctrine but because all dogmatic definitions by Councils were apt to arouse controversy in the Church. Even in the case of the early Councils, which had been necessary because of heresy, there had been a great deal of confusion and dissension in the wake of their decisions. In the case of papal infallibility there were none of those "heretical questionings" that, Newman had pointed out in the *Apologia,* "have been transmuted by the living power of the Church into salutary truths."[13] Even at this early stage of the proceedings Newman was well aware that Councils can have effects which are not intended. For by defining the infallibility of the pope the Council would not merely be saying something about the pope; the definition would inevitably have wider repercussions on the Church. Apart from the enormous controversy it would generate, it would necessarily lead "to an alteration of the *elementary constitution* of the Church" in so far as it would encourage popes to act independently of the bishops.[14]

This is not the place to consider Newman's particular objections to a definition by the Council. But his objection to its opportuneness does have a more general significance. His caution about precipitate changes or developments was aimed at the Ultramontanes — "We do not move at railroad pace in theological matters, even in the 19th century" — but has a wider relevance for own times. He insisted that the Church "moves as a whole," as a communion

---

[13] *Apo.*, 237.
[14] *LD*, xxiv: 377.

rather than an ideology, has "no right rudely to wipe out the history of centuries..." It was particularly serious if "a grave dogmatic question was being treated merely as a move in ecclesiastical politics."[15] In the contemporary Church it has sometimes seemed that those pressing for the ordination of women, for instance, have been more concerned with feminism than doctrine.

Although Newman was scandalized by the intrigues of the Ultramontanes, he could not agree with the German church historian Döllinger that their behaviour in any way affected the validity of the Council. Such political manoeuvring was unfortunately a feature of Councils. The fact was that General Councils had "ever been times of great *trial*" and "the conduct of individuals who composed them was no measure of their result."[16] History showed that Councils had "generally two characteristics — a great deal of violence and intrigue on the part of the actors in them, and a great resistance to their definitions on the part of portions of Christendom."[17]

When the definition was finally passed, Newman immediately began to adumbrate a theology of reception. A large minority of bishops had absented themselves in protest from the final vote, and in the absence of a "moral" unanimity there was some doubt about its validity. But if there was no persistent, united opposition on their part to the definition, and, most important of all, "if the definition is eventually received by the whole body of the faithful, then too it will claim our assent by the force of the great dictum, 'Securus judicat orbis terrarum'."[18] This aphorism of St. Augustine, which had made such a deep impression on Newman in the summer of 1839, shortly after the first blow, once again rang

[15] *LD*, xxv: 93, 95.
[16] *LD*, xxv: 158.
[17] *LD*, xxvi: 281.
[18] *LD*, xxv: 165.

insistently in his ears. "The universal Church is in its judgments secure of truth" was Newman's own free translation.[19] This meant that "the general acceptance, judgment of Christendom" was not only "the broad principle, by which all acts of the rulers of the Church are ratified," but also "the ultimate guarantee of revealed truth."[20]

As soon as it became clear that the definition was the mind of the Church, Newman began to reflect, pragmatically as ever, on what was now a *fait accompli*. Before he had had no illusions about the human side of Councils; now he was ready to admit that "a General Council may be hampered and hindered by the action of infidel governments upon a weak or time-serving episcopate." The argument that papal authority required strengthening was not lost on Newman, who was by now prepared to admit: "It is... better that the individual command of Christ to Peter to teach the nations, and to guard the Christian structure of society, should be committed to his undoubted successor. By this means there will be no more of those misunderstandings out of which Jansenism and Gallicanism have arisen, and which in these latter days have begotten here in England the so-called Branch Theory..."[21]

Although, however, the actual wording of the definition, which was weaker than the Ultramontanes had wanted, was quite unexceptionable and even desirable in theory, still the reality was that, "considered in its effects both upon the Pope's mind and that of his people, and in the power of which it puts him in practical possession, it is nothing else than shooting Niagara." The proceedings at the Council were certainly scandalous but that was no excuse for Döllinger and others to exaggerate what had actually been defined.

[19] *Essays Critical and Historical*, ii: 101.
[20] *LD*, xxv: 165, 172.
[21] *LD*, xxv: 259.

The important thing, Newman urged in his private correspondence, was patience: "Remedies spring up naturally in the Church, as in nature, if we wait for them." The definition could not simply be considered by itself; the context, or rather lack of context, was very important, for the "definition was taken out of its order — it would have come to us very differently, if those preliminaries about the Church's power had first been passed, which... were intended."[22] If the Council, which had been cut short prematurely by political events and suspended indefinitely by Pius IX, did reassemble, it would hopefully "occupy itself in other points" which would "have the effect of qualifying and guarding the dogma."[23] If this was not to be, then the Council would be completed and modified by another Council, as had happened before in the history of the Church. It was characteristic that Newman turned for guidance to the history of the early Church:

> Another consideration has struck me forcibly, and that is, that, look-ing at early history, it would seem as if the Church moved on to the perfect truth by various successive declarations, alternately in con-trary directions, and thus perfecting, completing, supplying each other. Let us have a little faith in her, I say. Pius is not the last of the Popes — the fourth Council modified the third, the fifth the fourth.... The late definition does not so much need to be undone, as to be completed. It needs *safeguards* to the Pope's possible acts — expla-nations as to the matter and extent of his power. I know that a vio-lent reckless party, had it its will, would at this moment define that the Pope's powers need no safeguards, no explanations — but there is a limit to the triumph of the tyrannical — Let us be patient, let us have faith, and a new Pope, and a re-assembled Council may trim the boat.[24]

---

[22] *LD*, xxv: 262.
[23] *LD*, xxv: 278.
[24] *LD*, xxv: 310.

Considering that Newman had consoled himself with the thought that there were advantages in popes doing what Councils had normally done in the past, and considering that after Vatican I it was widely believed that there would be no need of future Councils, this letter is a remarkable prophecy of Vatican II. And, of course, what Newman says about the way in which the Church moves "alternately in contrary directions" has application not only to Vatican II, which was hardly a linear process of movement from Vatican I, whatever the extreme Ultramontanes of the time may have assumed or hoped about the eventual reinforcing and strengthening of the definition. It may also apply to post-Vatican II developments. Post-Vatican II progressives may find that their scenario for the future is as unrealistic as any Ultramontane hopes that may have been entertained for the development of the definition of papal infallibility.

The letter quoted above represents the view that Newman was forming, above all on the basis of his knowledge of the Church's early Councils. He continued to insist that the first defined Catholic dogmas "were not struck off all at once but piecemeal — one Council did one thing, another a second — and so the whole dogma was built up." It was precisely because "the first portion of it looked extreme" that controversies arose which led to subsequent Councils which "*explained* and *completed* what was first done."[25] From our vantage point, it is an exact prediction of the Second Vatican Council's constitution on the Church, *Lumen Gentium,* where the papal primacy is moderated by its being placed within the context of the apostolic college of bishops: the pope is the head of but still a member of the college and not exalted above it.

What Newman has to say about the inevitable confusion Vatican I had caused applies even more to the effect of Vatican II

[25] *LD*, xxv: 330.

on the internal life of the Church. True, no dogmatic definitions of the magnitude of papal infallibility were passed, but the actual consequences of the second reforming Council were much more disruptive on a large scale. After all, in a real sense Vatican II brought the era of the Tridentine Church to a close, whereas Vatican I did no such thing. Certainly a "new" dogma had serious theological repercussions: "intellectual scrutiny" was required of "the Vatican definitions, and their sense will have to be wrought out" — but, Newman stipulates, "in friendly controversy" — words which have an obvious application in the era we live in. Catholic theology had absorbed Trent; it now had another Council to digest. Theologians had had three hundred years to explain and interpret Trent — but "now we are new born children, the birth of the Vatican Council... We do not know what exactly we hold — what we may grant, what we must maintain."[26] These words apply at least as much to the period immediately after Vatican II, and indeed even later. The fact was, Newman pointed out, that Councils "generally acted as a lever, displacing and disordering portions of the existing theological system," often being followed by acrimonious controversies within the Church.[27]

It is, again, paradoxical that the more Newman saw reason to dread Councils, the more the papacy appealed to him. Certainly, if the proceedings of Councils "are to be the measure of their authority, they are, with few exceptions, a dreary, unlovely phenomenon in the Church."[28] It is striking how the more negatively Newman felt about Councils, the more positive he was towards the Petrine office: "The more one examines the Councils, the less satisfactory they are — [but] the less satisfactory they, the more majestic and

---

[26] *LD*, xxvi: 59-60.
[27] *LD*, xxvi: 76.
[28] *LD*, xxvi: 120.

trust-winning, and the more imperatively necessary, is the action of the Holy See."[29]

Turning now to the question of the reception, in the sense of the interpretation, of councils, Newman had already pointed out, before the definition of papal infallibility, in a private letter of March 1870, that even if the Council did decide that the infallibility of the pope should be defined, that would still not rule out the necessity of interpretation of his definitions. The same was true of a Council's definitions, which — just as "lawyers explain acts of Parliament" — had to be explained by theologians. Obvious as the fact might be, there was a serious conclusion that Newman does not hesitate to draw from it: "Hence, I have never been able to see myself that the ultimate decision rests with any but the general Catholic intelligence." It was after all implied by Newman's beloved maxim: "Securus judicat orbis terrarum."[30] He certainly did not mean that definitions were not authentic until "received" by the whole Church; only that the validity of definitions had to be recognized by the Church — if, for example, the pope went insane no solemn teaching by him could be accepted. Eventually the definition of papal infallibility would look rather different than had first appeared to people at the time.

For "the voice of the Schola Theologorum, of the whole Church diffusive" would "in time make itself heard," and "Catholic instincts and ideas" would in the end "assimilate and harmonize" it into the wider context of Catholic beliefs. As time went on, too, theologians would "settle the force of the wording of the dogma, just as the courts of law solve the meaning and bearing of Acts of Parliament."[31] While it was hardly more than common sense that

[29] *LD*, xxviii: 172.
[30] *LD*, xxv: 71.
[31] *LD*, xxv: 447.

ultimately the only way in which the solemn teachings of popes
and Councils could be authenticated was by the acceptance and
recognition by the Church that they were indeed what they pur-
ported to be, nevertheless their interpretation involved necessarily
the technicalities of theology: the meaning of dogmatic propositions was not self-evident, but they were "always made with the
anticipation and condition of this lawyer-like, or special-pleader-
like, action of the intellect upon them."[32] The fact is, Newman
pointed out, all human statements require interpretation. And in
defining doctrine, popes and Councils enjoyed an "active infallibility," but more was involved in the infallibility of the Church
than that, since a *"passive infallibility"* belonged to the whole body
of the Catholic faithful, who had to determine the force and
meaning of these doctrinal teachings, although naturally the chief
responsibility for this lay with the theologians, whose discussions
and investigations assured a clear distinction between "theological truth" and mere "theological opinion." The differences
between theologians maintained "liberty of thought," while their
consensus on points of dogma was "the safeguard of the infallible
decisions of the Church."[33] Infallibility belonged to the whole
Church —again, "Securus judicat orbis terrarum." It is clear all
these points apply also to the Second Vatican Council even though
it was not a dogmatic Council like Vatican I. And they help to show
how naive and superficial was the idea after Vatican II that all that
had to be done was for the decrees to be "implemented," as though
the texts spoke for themselves and implementation was a simple
straightforward matter. Newman by no means ruled out the possibility of what he called "a false interpretation" of the definition of
papal infallibility. And, considering the "creeping infallibility" that

[32] *LD*, xxvi: 35.
[33] *LD*, xxvii: 338.

followed Vatican I, he was not so far off the mark. But in that event, he predicted, "another Leo will be given us for the occasion." The reference is to Pope St. Leo's Council of Chalcedon, which, "without of course touching the definition" of the preceding Council of Ephesus, "trimmed the balance of doctrine by completing it."[34] Newman's prophecy came true with Pope John XXIII. Newman could have predicted the dissensions within the Catholic Church since Vatican II. As he knew only too well, one of the "disadvantages of a General Council, is that it throws individual units through the Church into confusion and sets them at variance."[35] He was not in the least surprised at the rise of the Old Catholics and the extremism of the only partially successful Ultramontane party. Similarly, neither the Lefebvrist schism nor the ultra-progressivist position in our own time would have caused Newman much surprise. If one may use crude, political labels, the "right" won at Vatican I and the "left" at Vatican II, but the extremists at both failed to achieve all that they wanted. Another similarity is that in the aftermath of both Councils it suited the extreme protagonists on both sides, both the partially victorious and the defeated, to exaggerate what had actually been decided by the respective Councils. This enabled both Döllinger and Lefebvre to claim that the Church had done a *volte-face* and abandoned its tradition. For Newman to appeal to history in this way against the Church's judgment was like using "private judgment" to interpret "Scripture against the voice of authority;" but if this was "unlawful," why should it "be lawful in the interpretation of history?" The Church certainly made use of history as it made use of Scripture, tradition, and reason, but ultimately what was important for a Catholic was "faith in the word of the Church." To both Döllinger and Lefebvre

---

[34] *Difficulties of Anglicans*, ii: 312. Hereafter cited as *Diff.*
[35] *LD*, xxvii: 240

Newman would only reiterate, "Securus judicat orbis Terrarum."[36] But at the same time he would have sympathized with Lefebvre as he did with Döllinger over the aggressive extremism of the opposite side. Newman criticized Manning for the extraordinary "rhetoric" he used over the infallibility issue, especially his pastoral letter of October 1870 which gave the impression that papal infallibility was unlimited.[37] I think he would have been at least as critical of Hans Küng and his party. Just as the extreme Ultramontanes did their best to encourage "creeping infallibility," so contemporary progressivists constantly appeal to "the spirit of Vatican II," but with scant regard for the actual text, let alone for those who happen to disagree with them as to the nature of what such a "spirit" might be.

It seems to me that Newman's reflections both at the time of and in the aftermath of Vatican I — reflections, I may say, which have received little attention, at least in their fullness — are of great interest for the contemporary Church as it seeks to interpret the meaning of Vatican II, as well as its significance for the development of Catholicism. Enough, I think, has been said to illustrate how superficial is any kind of understanding which assumes that the meaning or "spirit" of the Council is patently obvious, rather than something which will only fully emerge in time and through the agency of various elements in the Church — certainly not, for example, simply through episcopal implementation, as was widely taken for granted in the years immediately following the Council.

In Newman's reflections on Councils and their aftermaths, there are in fact two different kinds of development he is talking about. The first kind is illuminated by one of his most telling images. It occurs in the first section of the first chapter of *An Essay on the*

---

[36] *Diff.*, ii: 312.
[37] *LD*, xxvii: 383; xxv: 230.

Development of Christian Doctrine, where Newman is speaking about the process of development in ideas. Pointing out that a living idea cannot be isolated "from intercourse with the world around," he argues that this contact is actually necessary "if a great idea is duly to be understood, and much more if it is to be fully exhibited." In Newman's terminology, Christianity is just such an "idea." There is an obvious objection to the argument: namely, that the further anything moves from its origin or source, the more likely it is to lose its pristine character. Conceding that certainly there is always the risk of an idea being corrupted by external forces, Newman nevertheless insists that, while "It is indeed sometimes said that the stream is clearest near the spring," this is not true of the kind of idea he is talking about.

> Whatever use may fairly be made of this image, it does not apply to the history of a philosophy or belief, which on the contrary is more equable, and purer, and stronger, when its bed has become deep, and broad, and full. It necessarily rises out of an existing state of things, and or a time savours of the soil. Its vital element needs disengaging from what is foreign and temporary...[38]

It is worth noting that the conclusion to this section contains perhaps the most quoted of all Newman's sayings, but since it is invariably cited out of context it is invariably misinterpreted. The famous words are: "In a higher world it is otherwise, but here below to live is to change, and to be perfect is to have changed often." Newman would certainly be horrified by the way in which this sentence is flourished by the kind of progressivist for whom all change is necessarily desirable. For far from being intended as a slogan for a progressivist agenda, it is in reality a deeply *conservative* point that Newman is making. But this is far from saying that

---

[38] *Essay on the Development of Christian Doctrine*, 39-40. Hereafter cited as *Dev.*

the words should bring comfort to reactionary or integralist Catholics. It is a dynamic not a static Catholicism that Newman has in mind. In terms of his thinking on the phenomenon of development, an idea like Catholicism has no alternative but to be dynamic unless it is to become ossified or to die. But there is another possibility to either living or dying, and that is to be corrupted. It is here that Newman rejects the progressivist alternative. For the sentence which precedes the celebrated aphorism and which is never quoted makes it crystal clear what kind of changing is intended: "It [that is, an idea] changes with them [that is, external circumstances] in order to remain the same."[39] This sentence, which is always ignored when the concluding sentence that follows it is quoted, is crucial for understanding the latter. And it sums up with admirable succinctness Newman's general theological stance, which is a *via media* between conservative and liberal Catholicism in the bad senses of reactionary and progressivist. On the one hand, the continuing identity of an idea is not conserved by remaining static; on the other hand, although it has to undergo change, this is not for the sake of change itself — if this were the case, then it would be the kind of change which Newman calls a corruption — but in order for the idea *to remain the same.* It is this kind of change which Newman terms development.

Now if Newman is correct in what he says about an idea such as a philosophy or belief becoming "more equable, and purer, and stronger" as it develops in the course of time, then this is a diagnosis which we can apply to Vatican II. The participants in and observers of that Council no doubt thought they knew very well what, for better or worse, the Council meant. Both Küng and Lefebvre had absolutely no doubt in their minds about how the Council was to be understood, and, paradoxically, like Döllinger

39 *Dev.*, 40.

and Manning, were closely in agreement about its meaning. In retrospect, we can see much better the very limited scope of the definition of papal infallibility and appreciate the accuracy of Newman's interpretation of it. But for both Döllinger and Manning the definition loomed very large indeed and signified far more than Catholic theology has since understood it to mean — an understanding which received the formal endorsement of Vatican II. In the case of Vatican II, it similarly suited both Küng and Lefebvre to exaggerate the revolutionary nature of the Council, even though the so-called revolution caused as much delight to the former as distress to the latter. If it is true — and indeed it has become something of a truism — to call Newman "the Father of Vatican II" because of the ways in which he anticipated the Council in his own theology,[40] then it is not unreasonable to apply the theology of Councils which he adumbrated at the time of Vatican I, together with his theology of development, to the question of the reception and interpretation of Vatican II, as well as to future possible developments. As Nicholas Lash puts it, while before the Second Vatican Council Newman was "still an occasionally suspect stranger, an outsider to the neo-scholastic world" of Catholic theology — we might add that he was considered much more dangerous in his own time — after the Council he became "its godfather and our guide into the strange territory that now lay before us."[41]

Taking Newman as our guide, then, we may legitimately use that passage in the *Essay on Development* in connection with the teaching of Vatican II and suggest that those critics, of whom Hans Küng

---

[40] See, e.g., Ian T. Ker, "Newman and the Postconciliar Church," *Newman Today*, ed. Stanley L. Jaki (San Francisco, CA: Ignatius Press, 1988) 121-141; Nicholas Lash, "Tides and Twilight: Newman since Vatican II," *Newman after a Hundred Years*, eds. Ian Ker and Alan G. Hill (Oxford: Clarendon Press, 1990) 447-464.

[41] Lash, "Tides and Twilight," 454.

is the most prominent, who lived through the Council and deplore the pontificate of John Paul II as a gross betrayal of Vatican II, may paradoxically be in a less good position to understand the real significance of the Council than they assume to be the case. The idea — or "spirit" — of Vatican II will grow "more equable, and purer, and stronger" if Newman's analysis is correct, as the "stream" moves away from "the spring" and "its bed has become deep, and broad, and full." Vatican II did not take place in a historical void; it actually met in a decade of enormous upheaval and change, a time of optimistic euphoria and a time of great moral and spiritual devastation. It took place in a period of revolution and inevitably "savoured" of "the soil" of the 1960s, that "existing state of things," to use Newman's words, out of which it arose. Assuming that Vatican II was an important Council, a Council which brought to an end the Tridentine era, then its "vital element needs disengaging from what is foreign and temporary." And on that note, it is worth recalling again how constantly after Vatican I Newman repeated that time is the great healer: "our duty is patience…" There was, it is true, a wait of nearly a hundred years, but patience had its reward in 1962. "Our wisdom is to keep quiet," Newman had written in a private letter of 1871, "not to make controversy, not to make things worse, but to pray that He, who before now has completed a first Council by a second, may do so now."[42]

This takes us on to the second kind of development that Newman speaks of in his mini-theology of Councils. For is not only a question of the meaning and significance of an "idea" like the theology of Vatican II becoming more luminous and focused as it is seen in retrospect in the developing life of the Church, but there is also the consideration that Councils open up further developments because of what they *don't* say or stress. Obviously, Vatican I and

[42] *LD*, xxv: 278.

Vatican II are very unlike in the matter of unfinished business which they left behind them, if only because the former was not allowed to finish its business. It is true, of course, that not everything that all the bishops at Vatican II wanted to discuss was on the agenda, but the fact remains that the Council did finish what it had formally intended to do and sat for four years compared with Vatican I which lasted less than a year.

Now whereas Newman's prediction that there would have to be another Council to fill out the incomplete ecclesiology of Vatican I was correct but not exactly startling in its penetration — when it comes to the completed Second Vatican Council, predicting what new directions the Church will move in is more problematic. There were and are many who see the future as simply a kind of continuation of Vatican II. But the Church cannot perpetually have the same priorities that that Council very reasonably had. In view of the definition of papal infallibility, it was essential that the Council should modify the Petrine primacy by placing it within the larger college of bishops. Similarly, the role of the laity, which Newman had vainly tried to stress, needed special emphasis. Again, the Council knew that the rise of the ecumenical movement called for a positive response by the Church. It was felt, too, that the time had come, as Newman himself had so often desiderated, for the Catholic Church to emerge from its splendid isolation from the modern world and engage in a dialogue with modern culture and thought. In an increasingly global world, Catholicism also needed to make contact with the world's other religions. Such were the kind of priorities at Vatican II, but to insist that they should remain at the top of the Church's agenda indefinitely would seem a strange form of progress.

In the event, "another Leo," to compare a small with a big intervention, was "given... for the occasion," when Pope Paul VI, nine years after the end of the Council, issued an urgent call for a new evangelization in *Evangelii Nuntiandi* (1974). Understandably, this was not on the agenda of the Council. But, to adapt some famous words of Newman, the Church would look foolish if it no longer had even enough members to engage in social issues of justice and peace, ecumenism, and the other kinds of dialogue that the Council had called for, and no less foolish if a preoccupation with its internal structures led to empty pews and few candidates to fill the manifold committees and commissions. As is well known. Pope John Paul II has made evangelization, often in typically dramatic ways, a major theme of his pontificate. Indeed, the Church has to move with the times and priorities do have to change, much to the dismay of both integralists resistant to all change and also, interestingly, of the so-called progressive wing of the Church (after all, no one is more reactionary than a successful revolutionary). The particular emphases of Vatican II had led to a perceptible weakening in the commitment to fulfil the Church's fundamental mandate to preach the gospel, and so "another Leo" was given "to trim the balance." But there have been other developments since the Council in reaction to the exaggerations which naturally follow from the specific themes of Vatican II. Thus the decision to include the Blessed Virgin Mary within the constitution on the Church rather than to devote a separate document to her caused a diminution of Marian piety, but there has been a very noticeable reaction to this from the devotional grassroots. Or again, the Council's teaching on the liturgy had the effect of downgrading traditional Eucharistic devotions, but in recent years these have experienced remarkable revival.

By way of a conclusion, I should like to draw attention to one quite unexpected post-conciliar phenomenon, which is vitally connected with the new evangelization, but which also exemplifies both the two kinds of Newmanian developments I have been talking about. I refer to the rise of the so-called new "ecclesial movements." For, on the one hand, these initiatives can be seen as representing a reaction against certain post-conciliar tendencies, and thus helping to restore a balance. But, on the other hand, they also may be viewed as a concrete realization of what I suggest will ultimately prove to be the most significant text of the Council.

One might say that, while the papacy emerged victorious out of Vatican I, at Vatican II the two elements in the Church which were given a high profile were the bishops and the laity. Indeed, after the Council many bishops gave the impression that they and the laity were now the key players in the life of the Church. Thanks, of course, to the pontificate of John Paul II the papacy refused to be, as it were, put down. The clergy were less fortunate, and at least some of the crisis in the priesthood can be attributed to the *de facto* marginalization of priests. But who were these "laity" to whom bishops increasingly turned to put on committees and commissions as well as to occupy paid jobs in the diocesan bureaucracy? They certainly didn't include the aged or children, who presumably belong to the ranks of the laity. Nor did they include the uneducated. In general, the new class of "laity" that emerged in the wake of Vatican II were articulate, middle-class Catholics.

The movements were very different. For a start, they were not inspired by bishops nor were they set up by diocesan committees or commissions. They came from the "bottom" rather than the "top." Significantly, they met with papal approval and encouragement under both Paul VI and John Paul II; on the other hand, bishops were often hostile or suspicious, and even more so the new class of episcopally approved laity. Moreover, the movements were by no means restricted to a particular section of the laity nor were they marked by any sort of ageism. From this point of view, the movements very definitely represented a reaction to an unbalanced post-conciliar tendency that was the human result of certain emphases in the Council.

However, there was another respect in which the movements seem to be a concrete manifestation of Vatican II ecclesiology. For it has to be underlined that it is strictly erroneous to call the new ecclesial movements *lay* movements, since priests, bishops, religious, as well as those lay members of the movements whose commitment to the charism and apostolate of the particular movement to which they belong marks them out as quasi-religious, even if canon law has not yet caught up with them, belong to them. What is so characteristic and significant about the movements is that they bring together the *baptised,* whatever their particular status in the Church, in a common if differentiated mission. The movements are not lay, but nor are they clerical, and it is in this respect they represent a novel phenomenon. Elsewhere,[43] in writing about Newman's *On Consulting the Faithful in Matters of Doctrine* — tellingly, often referred to as *On Consulting the* Laity *in Matters of Doctrine* — I pointed out that, although Newman certainly uses the term laity in the famous article — he could hardly help doing so in the highly clericalized Church with which he was writing — nevertheless the historical examples he gives from the fourth century make it abundantly clear that the "faithful" comprised not only laity but also "presbyters," "holy virgins," and "monks," in other words priests and religious. It was not just the laity but the faithful or baptized Christians — whatever their canonical status in the Church — who upheld the orthodox faith against the Arian heresy despite the failure of the body of the episcopate to stand firm. I also referred to a note Newman added to an appendix to the third edition of *The Arians of the Fourth Century* when he republished it in 1871. This note contains part of the

---

[43] Ian Ker, "Newman on the *Consensus Fidelium* as 'the voice of the infallible Church'," *Newman and the Word,* ed. Terrence Merrigan and Ian T. Ker (Louvain-Paris-Sterling/Grand Rapids, MI: Peeters Press/W. B. Eerdmans, 2000) 69-89.

article, together with some amendments and additions, including a remarkable sentence, which not even G. K. Chesterton at his most paradoxical could outdo: "And again, in speaking of the laity, I speak inclusively of their parish-priests (so to call them), at least in many places..."[44]

I then compared Newman's article with the Vatican II constitution on the Church, *Lumen Gentium,* where there is indeed a special chapter devoted to the laity. But the interesting aspect of this chapter is the virtual absence of any Scriptural or Patristic sources, which, of course, is not surprising as the early Church had not yet become clericalized and so there was no need to employ the concept. In the first two chapters, on the contrary, where the Council sets out its essential and fundamental understanding of the Church, the text not only bristles with Scriptural and Patristic references, but also avoids speaking of the Church as though it consisted of clergy and laity. The first chapter doesn't even employ the terms, although it does single out "the grace of the apostles" as "the primary" of the gifts of the Spirit. And the second chapter deals with the "ministerial or hierarchical priesthood" simply in terms of the specific sacrament of holy orders among the various sacraments which build up the "common priesthood of the faithful;" again the chapter studiously avoids talking of the Church in the usual terms of clergy and laity.

In that first section of the first chapter of the *Essay on Development,* Newman says that if one was looking for the "'leading idea'... of Christianity," round which other ideas could be grouped simply "for convenience," then he would "call the Incarnation the central aspect of Christianity." And later in the book he refers to the Incarnation as "the central truth of the Gospel."[45] I have no

---

[44] *Arians of the Fourth Century,* 445.

[45] *Dev.,* 35-36, 324.

doubt that if Newman could have been asked the same question about Vatican II, he would have said that its teaching on the idea or nature of the Church in those first two foundational chapters of *Lumen Gentium* is the central teaching of a Council which was overwhelmingly an ecclesial Council, a Council concerned with the Church, its internal components and structures, its liturgy, its relationship with other Christians, non-Christians, and the world.

But the fact is that these two crucial chapters which marked a radical return to the Scriptural and Patristic understanding of the Church as primarily not hierarchical or institutional but sacramental, the mystical body of Christ, the communion of those who have received the Holy Spirit in baptism, have been largely ignored in favour of the later two chapters on the bishops and the laity. It is hardly surprising that these two more topical chapters received more attention at the time, but in the long run it is surely the first two chapters which do not seem to be saying anything very new or interesting which will prove to be revolutionary — but only in the sense of being utterly traditional in returning the Church to its roots.

What is so significant about the new movements is that they provide flesh and blood to these two chapters. For they are not traditional religious orders or lay associations but communities of the baptized who have received the "varied hierarchic and charismatic gifts" which the Holy Spirit bestows. But if the movements make the central meaning of *Lumen Gentium* clearer and stronger, they also represent another kind of development in Newman's terms, a reaction against both a clericalized and a laicized Church. It is not surprising that both wings of the Church find them a disturbing and suspicious phenomenon. But if, in spite of not being inspired or directed by either the hierarchy or the "official" laity they are the work of the Spirit, then they may throw a lot of light on the meaning, not to say the spirit, of Vatican II.

DISPENSATIONS OF GRACE
NEWMAN ON THE SACRAMENTAL MEDIATION OF SALVATION

Geoffrey WAINWRIGHT

A Strange Guest

As an ecclesial child of John Wesley, I am a strange guest at this celebration of the 200th anniversary of John Henry Newman's birth. Newman disliked his Oxford predecessor of the previous century: he found in "Westley," whom he knew from Robert Southey's biography, an "exceeding self confidence" and "a black self will, a bitterness of religious passion, which is very unamiable."[1] Moreover, in his own Anglo-Catholic days Newman ranked contemporary Methodism with the Dissenters as a blot on the religious landscape of England. Nevertheless, he then and later managed a few half-way positive comments on early and subsequent Methodism, though usually taking back with the other hand what he had given with the one.

For our assigned theme of the sacramental mediation of salvation, it is of particular interest that Newman viewed the rise of Methodism as having filled a vacuum in the life of the Church of England. In 1835 he lamented the loss of "the Sacrament ... such as it was in the Primitive Church, as Ridley managed to keep it, as Andrew[e]s and Laud maintained it, and as the Nonjurors enjoyed it — the presence of Christ in the Church for doctrine and grace —

[1] Letter of January 19, 1837 to his sister Jemima, Mrs. John Mozley, *LD*, vi: 16.

a continual revelation of the Incarnation. When the last mentioned [i.e. the Nonjurors] was expelled from the Church, the natural consequence followed... They took with them all the rich furniture of the Sanctuary; and the spiritual principle of Christianity, unable to live off the husks of Kennett, Hoadley, Clarke and the rest, burst forth first into Methodism, then into the Evangelical School, which has the ardour and some of the depth of the Old Catholic Doctors, without their reverence, sanctity, and majesty."[2] In his historical sketches written around that time for the *British Magazine*, Newman said that Methodism had "carried off many a man" who aspired after the "piety and holiness" that the early monastic orders had catered for.[3] In his Lenten lectures at the London Oratory in 1850, Newman could tell Anglo-Catholics that "if you wish to find the shadow and the suggestion of the supernatural qualities which make up the notion of a Catholic Saint, to Wesley you must go, and such as him" (though "personally I do not like him, if it were merely for deep self-reliance and self-conceit"). Likewise, he went on, Wesley and his companions, "starting amid ridicule at Oxford, with fasting and praying in the cold night air, then going about preaching, reviled by the rich and educated, and pelted and dragged to prison by the populace, and converting thousands from sin to God's service," might evoke the great Catholic missionaries of former times — "were it not for their pride and eccentricity, their fanatical doctrine and untranquil devotion." In any case, if Anglo-Catholics wanted to argue from the "sensible effects of supernatural grace" among them to the place of the Church of England in the Catholic Church, then they should be aware that the Methodists displayed "more remarkable phenomena in their history, symptomatic of the presence of grace among them, than you can show in

[2] Letter of March 16, 1835 to James Stephen, *LD*, v: 47.
[3] From "Demetrias" in *HS,* ii: 164-165.

yours."[4] In the face of secularistic loss of faith, Newman could in 1869 opine that the Wesleyans were "more likely to make a stand against infidelity than any religious body in England" — "narrow-minded, self-sufficient, and conceited" as they were.[5] But enough: I will forget the rather grudging character of Newman's appreciation for Wesleyanism and his distaste for its eponymous founder. I had better resist replying in kind, given not only Newman's notorious sensitivity to personal affront but also his brilliant wit and the sharpness of his pen and his tongue; for after all I hope one day to meet him. Instead, I will behave professionally as an ecumenically-minded systematic theologian, a century and a half after Newman's time.

The structure of my reflections on the sacramental mediation of salvation will be as follows. In a first part, I will look most generally at what Newman, in his philosophy of religion, called "the sacramental principle," whereby the phenomena of nature and history bear the revelation of God. In a second and directly consequent part, I will go into Newman's ecclesiology of the visible, nay the tangible, Church. Third will come notice of Newman's christology as entailing a very "concrete" understanding of Christ ("concrete" is a favourite word of his in many contexts). A brief dip into Newman's epistemology — or at least into his semiotics to see how he relates words, deeds, and things — will lead finally into "the sacraments properly so called," as Newman presents them.[6]

---

[4] *Diff.*, i: 88-91.

[5] Letter of August 16, 1869 to E. B. Pusey, in *LD*, xxiv: 126-127.

[6] Ian Ker, *John Henry Newman: A Biography* (Oxford/New York: Oxford University Press, 1988). As a novice in Newman matters, I have been richly instructed by Ian Ker's magnificent biography of our subject. Besides *Tract 90* and the *Apologia Pro Vita Sua*, which used to be staples in any course on nineteenth-century English Church history, I knew as a theologian such major writings as the *Lectures on the Prophetical Office*, the *Essay on the Development of Doctrine*, and the *Essay in Aid of a Grammar of Assent*. But to Dr. Ker I owe my introduction

The Sacramental Principle

At three points early in the *Apologia* Newman speaks in a broad sense of a sacramental economy, or more precisely "the sacramental system" and "the sacramental principle." About the year 1823 he had read Bishop Joseph Butler's classic *Analogy of Religion* (1736), where he was struck, as its readers usually are, by "its inculcation of a visible Church, the oracle of truth and a pattern of sanctity, of the duties of external religion, and of the historical character of Revelation;" but Newman gained from his reading a further particular point, namely: "The very idea of an analogy between the separate works of God leads to the conclusion that the system which is of less importance is economically or sacramentally connected with the more momentous system."[7] The connection between the different members of an analogy — which is what Newman means in this first passage by systems — is itself in a second passage called "the sacramental system." John Keble's *Christian Year*, published in 1827, brought home to Newman what he "had learned from Butler, though recast in the creative mind of [his] new master;" for Keble's poems taught him "the sacramental system," namely "the doctrine that material phenomena are both the types and the instruments of real things unseen — a doctrine which embraces in its fulness, not only what Anglicans, as well as

not only to Newman's engagement with Henry Hart Milman's *History of Christianity* and Sir John Seeley's *Ecce Homo* but even to Newman's *Lectures on Justification* of 1838, which provide vital clues to what he respectively rejected or affirmed in the sacramental doctrines of "Protestantism" and "Catholicism;" and Ker's familiarity with the *Letters and Diaries* has provided me with some quotable tidbits as well as innumerable chuckles and bedazzled admiration at Newman's treatment of events great and small. My deep indebtedness to Ker's book, especially for references to follow up in Newman's *Letters and Diaries*, is here acknowledged once and for all.

7 *Apo.*, 22-23.

Catholics, believe about Sacraments properly so called; but also the article of 'the Communion of Saints'; and likewise the Mysteries of the faith."[8] In a third passage, this "sacramental system" is designated by Newman "the mystical or sacramental principle," which he rejoiced to find around 1830-1831 in his readings in the pre-Nicene Alexandrian Fathers, who spoke of "the various Economies or Dispensations of the Eternal." This third locus in the *Apologia* is especially important for several reasons: it makes the natural world, human culture, and religious history all part of the sacramental system; it introduces the notion, under God, of pagan, Jewish and Christian "dispensations;" it allows for a gradual divine revelation, whereby even the earthly Church and her sacraments are transcended by a future and heavenly reality. Newman's text must be quoted in full as he expounds the Alexandrians to mean that

the exterior world, physical and historical, was but the manifestation to our senses of realities greater then itself. Nature was a parable: Scripture was an allegory: pagan literature, philosophy, and mythology, properly understood, were but a preparation for the Gospel. The Greek poets and sages were in a certain sense prophets; for "thoughts beyond their thought to those high bards were given." There had been a directly divine dispensation granted to the Jews; but there had been in some sense a dispensation carried on in favour of the Gentiles. He who had taken the seed of Jacob for His elect people had not therefore cast the rest of mankind out of His sight. In the fulness of time both Judaism and Paganism had come to nought; the outward framework, which concealed yet suggested the Living Truth, had never been intended to last, and it was dissolving under the beams of the Sun of Justice which shone behind it and through it. The process of change had been slow; it had been done not rashly, but by rule and measure, "at sundry times and in divers manners," first one disclosure and then another, till the whole evangelical

8 *Ibid.*, 29.

doctrine was brought into full manifestation. And thus room was made for the anticipation of further and deeper disclosures, of truths still under the veil of the letter, and in their season to be revealed. The visible world still remains without its divine interpretation; Holy Church in her sacraments and her hierarchical appointments, will remain, even to the end of the world, after all but a symbol of those heavenly facts which fill eternity. Her mysteries are but the expressions in human language of truths to which the human mind is unequal.[9]

The "sacramental principle," so understood in Newman's "philosophy of religion," raises systematic and ecumenical questions in at least three connections: the material reality of the Christian sacraments; the value of other religions for salvation; and the historical and eschatological scope of the ecclesial dispensation.

First, the material reality of the Christian sacraments. In the passage quoted from the *Apologia* in reference to Butler's *Analogy*, Newman avows that he "inclined as a boy" to the theory of "the unreality of material phenomena," which he regards as "an ultimate resolution" to the notion of a graded analogical relationship among the various works of God. Note, please, "*an* ultimate resolution;" and note that Newman here, and again in the passage in reference to Keble's *Christian Year*, appears to distance himself from radical Idealism. Nevertheless, Newman's epistolary comment on "Berkeleyism," cited at these points by Martin Svaglic in his edition of the *Apologia*, is intriguing: "To what extent Berkeley denied the existence of the external world I am not aware; nor do I mean to go so far myself (far from it) as to deny the existence of matter, though I should deny that *what we saw* was more than accidents of it."[10] When a Protestant runs across the word "accidents"

---

[9] *Ibid.*, 36-37. The line of verse cited stems from Keble's *Christian Year*, no. XXVII, "Third Sunday in Lent."

[10] *Ibid.*, 488, 497, citing a letter of May 18, 1834 to Jemima Newman, now in *LD*, iv: 253.

in such a connection, his suspicious mind leaps philosophically to "hylomorphism" and theologically to "transubstantiation." Now that is a doctrine which gave Newman himself some trouble. In *Tract 90* he dismissed "objections against 'substance,' 'nature,' 'change,' 'accidents,' and the like" as "more or less questions of words;" but that was only to leave room for saying that those objections failed to capture "the great offence which we find in the received Roman view of this sacred doctrine" — and he cited doctrinal and theological texts of Roman origin that spoke of Christ's eucharistic presence in a "carnal" or, less crudely, "local" sense.[11] In the same year of 1841, he wrote to Ambrose Lisle Phillipps that the doctrine of transubstantiation was not "primitive."[12] But listen to Newman in the *Apologia* on the "position of my mind" since 1845:

> People say that the doctrine of Transubstantiation is difficult to believe; I did not believe the doctrine till I was a Catholic. I had no difficulty in believing it, as soon as I believed that the Catholic Roman Church was the oracle of God, and that she had declared this doctrine to be part of the original revelation. It is difficult, impossible, to imagine, I grant; — but how is it difficult to believe? ...
> For myself, I cannot indeed prove it, I cannot tell *how* it is; but I say, "Why should it not be? What's to hinder it? What do I know of substance or matter? Just as much as the greatest philosophers, and that is nothing at all." ... The Catholic doctrine leaves phenomena alone. It does not say that the phenomena go; on the contrary, it says that they remain; nor does it say that the same phenomena are in several

---

[11] "Tract 90" (1841), edited in 1877 in *VM*, ii: 315-322 ("Transubstantiation").

[12] Letter of September 12, 1841 to Ambrose Lisle Phillipps, 12 Sept. 1841, in *LD*, viii: 270. In the *Essay on the Development of Doctrine* Newman implied that the Real Presence confessed in the ante-Nicene fathers had benefited from later doctrinal clarification (Introduction, paragraphs 17-19; 23-27).

places at one. It deals with what no one on earth knows any thing about, the material substances themselves.[13]

Here we have Newman correcting his earlier "misunderstanding" of the Roman doctrine such as he had presented it in his 1838 *Letter to the Margaret Professor of Divinity*: "The Roman Church, we know, considers that the elements of Bread and Wine depart or are taken away on Consecration, and that the Body and Blood of Christ take their place. This is the doctrine of Transubstantiation; and in consequence they hold that what is seen, felt, and tasted, is not Bread and Wine but Christ's Flesh and Blood, though the former look, feel, and taste remains. This is what neither our Church, nor any of the late maintainers of her doctrine on the subject, even dreams of holding."[14] But, granted the reverent agnosticism about the "how" of the Presence in the passage from the *Apologia*, still it may be wondered whether it is proper to be quite so blasé about "material substances" when one is *tant soit peu* inclined to Idealism. Admittedly, the Roman doctrine of transubstantiation is unique to the eucharist among the sacraments; but therein may reside precisely the problem. When the twenty-eighth of the English Articles of Religion charges that the doctrine of transubstantiation "overthroweth the nature of a sacrament," part of the accusation must surely reside in a fear for the substantial integrity of the bread and wine (no such threat occurs with the water of baptism); and annihilationist accounts of the change in the eucharistic elements seem to lead in the direction of either docetism or pantheism (especially when, as in the writings of a Teilhard de Chardin, they are projected onto a cosmic and eschatological screen).

---

[13] *Apo.*, 215.

[14] "Letter to the Margaret Professor of Divinity," in *VM*, ii: 237. Newman's footnote of 1877 adds regarding his 1838 account of the Roman doctrine: "This is not accurate."

Ecumenically, stubborn controversy still surrounds the eucharistic Presence. In the Faith and Order text on *Baptism, Eucharist and Ministry* (1982), our statement that "the Church confesses Christ's real, living and active presence in the eucharist" met with very wide acceptance; but in our original commentary we had been obliged to recognize that churches differ over the relation between the presence of Christ and the bread and wine, and to say that "the decision remains for the churches whether this difference can be accommodated within the convergence formulated in the text." The official responses from the churches on all sides made clear that this was not the case.[15]

Now to the second kind of question arising in connection with Newman's "sacramental principle," that of "other religions." On his first visit to Sicily in February 1833 Newman had been impressed by the hilltop ruins of the solitary temple of Egesta: "Such was the genius of early Greek worship, grand in the midst of error;"[16] and he had viewed the whole island as "so beautiful and so miserable that it is an emblem of its own past history, i.e. the history of heathen countries, being a most noble record stone over the grave of high hopes and aims, pride, sin, and disappointment."[17] For our question it is at least interesting that Newman attended Mass, on the feast of the Annunciation in that same year, in the lovely Roman church whose very title indicates that it is built over a pagan site, Santa Maria sopra Minerva.[18]

---

[15] *Baptism, Eucharist and Ministry* (Geneva: World Council of Churches, 1982) 12 (paragraph E 13 and commentary); see also Geoffrey Wainwright, "The Eucharist in the Churches' Responses to the Lima Text," *One in Christ* 25 (1989) 53-74. As one of the original authors of *BEM*, I continue to adopt a certain proprietary style in speaking of the document.

[16] Letter of February 19, 1833 to Jemima Newman, in *LD*, iii: 219.

[17] Letter of March 14, 1833 to George Ryder, in *Ibid.*, 248.

[18] Letters of March 25, 1833 to his mother, in *Ibid.*, 266-268.

In his *Arians of the Fourth Century* Newman described the "Dispensation of Paganism" as a "vague and uncertain family of religious truths, originally from God, but sojourning without the sanction of miracle, or a definite home, as pilgrims up and down the world, and discernable and separable from the corrupt legends with which they are mixed, by the spiritual mind alone;" and the Christian apologist or missionary will, says Newman, follow St. Paul at Athens in "seek[ing] some points in the existing superstitions as the basis of his own instructions, instead of indiscriminately condemning and discarding the whole assemblage of heathen opinions and practices; and he will address his hearers, not as men in a state of actual perdition, but as being in imminent danger of 'the wrath to come,' because they are in bondage and ignorance, and probably under God's displeasure, that is, the vast majority of them are so in fact; but not necessarily so, from the very circumstance of their being heathen. And while he strenuously opposes all that is idolatrous, immoral, and profane, in their creed, he will profess to be leading them on to perfection, and to be recovering and purifying, rather than reversing the essential principles of their belief."[19] In his review of Milman's *History of Christianity*, Newman averred that "from the beginning the Moral Governor of the world has scattered the seeds of truth far and wide over its extent; that these have variously taken root, and grown up as in the wilderness, wild plants indeed but living; and hence that ... the philosophies and religions of men have their life in certain true ideas, though they are not directly divine;" and "the Church [has] from the first looked round upon the earth, noting and visiting the doctrines she found there." Her dealing with them has been discriminating — "claiming to herself what they said rightly, correcting their errors, supplying their defects,

---

[19] *Arians*, 80-81, 83-84.

completing their beginnings, expanding their surmises, and thus gradually by means of them enlarging the range and refining the sense of her own teaching."[20]

That delicately shaded policy allows for more nuances than the five "typical" attitudes towards the relation between "Christ and Culture" noted by H. Richard Niebuhr in his 1951 book of that title. On the one hand, it has the advantage of permitting Christians to use discrimination in their estimate of the various particular elements in societies outside the Church. Assuming, on the other hand, that a "religion," like a "culture," meets T. S. Eliot's definition as "a whole way of life," then each element within it will be coloured by the entire system and its place in it; so that a total grasp of that religion or culture is also needed. These tensions reach tangible expression when it comes to the ritual performance of the Christian sacraments. In his classic study of *The Early Liturgy to the Time of Gregory the Great* (1959), Josef Andreas Jungmann argued that the Church took over features from pagan cults only when these had become no longer a threat but were mere empty husks. In the *Essay on the Development of Doctrine*, Newman argued that the early Church's assimilative power — its success in "convert[ing] heathen appointments into spiritual rites and usages," in "purifying," "transmuting" and "grafting" them into "a system which is grace and truth" without itself being "infected" by them (ay, there's the rub) — was the note of a true development; and the Church's exercise of a discretionary power in these ways was an indication that "the Church has been entrusted with the dispensation of grace."[21]

Judgments are required in what is now usually called liturgical inculturation and acculturation. In modern times — it was certainly

---

[20] "Milman's View of Christianity," *Ess.*, ii: 231-232.
[21] *Essay on the Development of Doctrine*, 355-356, 368-380.

still the case during my own years as a missionary in French West Africa — Catholics have on the whole been more ready than Protestants to engage in what we then knew as "indigenization." True, the Bangalore Centre's religiously assimilative *Orders of the Mass for India* were rejected by Rome, while the dioceses of Zaïre received approval of a Missal that stressed christological mediation in all God's doings with the world;[22] but it may be generally fair to place Roman Catholicism under Niebuhr's type that looks for a Christian purification or sanation of cultures or their religions, while magisterial Protestantism — whether Lutheran or, say, Barthian — fits under "Christ and culture in paradox." Current theological debates seem to cross confessional lines: John Hick and Paul Knitter, two leading proponents of religious pluralism, come from Protestant and Catholic backgrounds respectively;[23] the World Methodist Council and Conference have just met in Brighton under the banner "Jesus — God's Way of Salvation," matching very nicely the position of the Roman Congregation for the Doctrine of the Faith in *Dominus Iesus* (2000) concerning Christ as the sole Saviour of the world. Much remains in favour of Newman's rather complex and dialectical understanding of the religions as *praeparatio evangelica*, which falls within the bounds of Vatican II's pronouncements on the matter.

The third kind of question in connection with Newman's "sacramental principle," broadly understood, concerns the historical and

---

[22] National Biblical Catechetical and Liturgical Centre, Bangalore, *New Orders of the Mass for India*, 1974 (these orders allowed for readings from Indian scriptures and made discreet references to animism, Hinduism, Buddhism, Jainism and Islam in the eucharistic prayer). *Missel romain pour les diocèses du Zaïre* (Kinshasa: Secrétariat général de la Conférence épiscopale du Zaïre, 1989).

[23] The names of Hick and Knitter are often linked on account of the symposium they edited, *The Myth of Christian Uniqueness: Toward a Pluralistic Theology of Religions* (Maryknoll, NY: Orbis Books, 1987).

eschatological scope of the ecclesial dispensation. "Holy Church in her sacraments and her hierarchical appointments," he wrote in the third and longest of our cited passages from the *Apologia*, "will remain, even to the end of the world, after all but a symbol of those heavenly facts which fill eternity." "But a symbol" is a turn of phrase that, since Rahner's splendidly concrete "Realsymbolik," we have come to suspect for its apparent diminution of the material sign. A similar hesitation might arise when Newman can be found saying, in an Oxford University Sermon of 1843, that "dogmas are, after all, but symbols of a Divine fact" and allowing that they "convey no true idea of Almighty God, but only an earthly one, gained from earthly figures," it being recognized in any case that "the senses do not convey to us any true idea of matter, but only an idea commensurate with sensible impressions." Somewhat more positively perhaps, Newman then comes round to allowing that "earthly figures and images" can give us "an approximation to the truth."[24]

Can we give a benign interpretation to Newman's version of the ecclesial stage in the history of salvation? Leaving aside for just a moment the controversial question of the composition of the Church, it is proper to note that ecumenical thinking on ecclesiology in the twentieth century reached a broad agreement concerning the nature of the earthly Church. Between the first coming of Christ and his awaited second advent, the Church is what the great ecumenist Lesslie Newbigin loved to call "the sign, first-fruit and instrument of the Kingdom."[25] Now that is sacramental language

[24] "The Theory of Developments in Religious Doctrine" (preached on February 2, 1843), in *Fifteen Sermons Preached before the University of Oxford* (third edition 1872), reprinted with an introduction by Mary Katherine Tillman (Notre Dame, IN: University of Notre Dame Press, 1997), in particular 332, 340.

[25] The triplet dates from Lesslie Newbigin's *The Household of God* (London: SCM Press, 1953), e.g. p. 146, and became coin of the realm in ecumenical

which recognizes not only the tension between "the already" and "the not yet" but also both the divine giftedness and the human responsibility of the Church. May we take Cardinal Newman's chosen epitaph — *Ex umbris et imaginibus in veritatem* — in that salvation-historical light? Certainly St. Ambrose held that the events under the Law were the shadow, that the sacraments of the Gospel are now the image, and that perfect truth belongs to Heaven, where Christ already is and where one day we shall be.[26]

If I have expressed doubts about Newman on material reality and have called attention, just now, to a certain apophaticism on his part (a theme which will resurface in connection with Newman's views on Revelation and Mystery), these two tendencies must both qualify and be qualified by his ecclesiology, to which I now turn in my search for the sacramental mediation of salvation according to Newman. Here it will be a question (systematically) of the nature of the Church, and a question (ecumenically) of the location of the Church.

The Ark of Salvation

In his review of Milman's *History of Christianity*, Newman restated his own sacramental principle as "the one great rule on which the Divine Dispensations with mankind have been and are conducted, that the visible world is the instrument, yet the veil, of

documents. Its occurrence and influence may be traced in my *Lesslie Newbigin: A Theological Life* (New York/Oxford: Oxford University Press, 2000).

[26] Ambrose, *In Ps.* 38, 25, PL 14:1051f.; *De officiis* I. 48, 238, PL 16, 94. On this kind of question, see my *Eucharist and Eschatology* (New York: Oxford University Press, ²1981). That Newman might occasionally slip into "realized eschatology" is suggested by the fact that Charles Reding, the hero of his novel *Loss and Gain*, could speak of his approach to the Catholic Church as "coming out of shadows into realities," 255.

the world invisible, — the veil, yet still partially the symbol and index: so that all that exists or happens visibly, conceals and yet suggests, and above all subserves, a system of persons, facts, and events beyond itself." In this light, "the world, the Bible, the Church, the civil polity, and man himself, are types, and, in their degree and place, representatives and organs of an unseen world, truer and higher than themselves." So, with regard to the Church: "The kingdom of Christ, though not of this world, yet is in the world, and has a visible, material, social shape."[27] What, more precisely, is this kingdom of Christ, and where is it to be found? In the same year of 1841 Newman phrased the question with incisive simplicity: "What and where is the Church?"[28]

"Christ," Newman told Mr. Gladstone by way of the Duke of Norfolk, "set up a visible society, or rather kingdom, for the propagation and maintenance of His religion, for a necessary home and refuge for His people."[29] And since, to put it at its simplest, Christ is axiomatically the Saviour, and the Atonement is the "central doctrine of the Gospel,"[30] the Church is, in a favourite image borrowed from St. Cyprian, the Ark of Salvation — which Newman came to identify exclusively with the Roman Catholic Church. What moved him to speak out to them, he told Anglicans in his London Oratory lectures of 1850, was "my intimate sense that the Catholic Church is the one ark of salvation, and my love for your souls;" the Roman Catholic Church was waiting to take in Anglo-Catholics who had "thrown themselves" from the "wreck" of the

---

[27] "Milman's View of Christianity," 192, 193, 196.

[28] "Private Judgment," *Ess.*, ii: 353.

[29] "A Letter Addressed to His Grace the Duke of Norfolk on Occasion of Mr. Gladstone's Recent Expostulation," *Diff.*, ii: 207.

[30] Letter of April 1, 1875, his nephew John Rickards Mozley, in *LD*, xxvii: 260.

Established Church upon "the waves" or were "clinging to its rigging" or "sitting in heaviness and despair upon its side."[31] Over against Anglican "branch" ecclesiologies and all talk of corporate reunion, Newman bluntly re-asserted that "the Roman Communion is the only True Church, the Ark of Salvation" and the only "religious body ... in which *is* salvation."[32] In the face of the rising tide of secularist infidelity, Newman in 1868 likened the Roman Catholic Church to Noah's Ark, which "did not hinder or destroy the flood but rode upon it, preserving the hopes of the human family within its fragile planks."[33] For all its own fragility, the "modern Roman Communion" remained "the heir and the image of the primitive Church," "almost like a photograph of the primitive Church."[34] The Catholic Church, being the "heir and representative" of "the ancient Church," is — Newman had said in the

---

[31] *Diff.*, i: 4.

[32] Letter of September 16, 1873 to Miss Rowe, in *LD*, xxvi: 364, and letter of December 20, 1881 to Mrs Lydia Rose Christie, in *LD*, xxx: 33-34. Newman could sustain the marine imagery in various ways: since the Reformation the (Roman Catholic) Church (in England) "has had to be piloted thro' very difficult straits and shallows with hidden rocks and without buoys and light-houses with next to no human means; and, though her Divine Guide has taken care she should not suffer material damage, and she has escaped in every peril, yet she has not much more than escaped; and it is natural and not very difficult for rival shipbuilders and shipowners to maintain that she had suffered" — thus a letter of March 12, 1875 to Ambrose Phillipps de Lisle, in *LD*, xxvii: 248. When already in 1857 Ambrose Lisle Phillipps, as he then was (he changed his name to Ambrose Phillipps de Lisle in 1862), had advocated a corporate reunion of the Church of England with Rome, Newman had remarked that "we did not pray for the conversion of the Church of England any more than we pray for the Fishmongers Company as such, because we did not allow its religious existence" — whatever may be the case with individual Anglicans or fishmongers; thus a letter of April 6, 1857 to E. H. Thompson, in *LD*, xxviii: 12.

[33] Letter of August 16, 1868 to E. B. Pusey, in *LD*, xxiv: 126.

[34] Letter of August 9, 1867 to E. B. Pusey, in *LD*, xxiii: 288, and letter of August 30, 1869 to Mrs Magdalene Helbert, in *LD*, xxiv: 325.

Brompton lectures of 1850 — the locus of Christianity as "an external fact, entering into, carried out in, indivisible from, the history of the world," having "a bodily occupation of the world" and constituting "one continuous fact or thing, the same from first to last."[35] As the First Vatican Council approached, Newman would speak of the Catholic Church as "the organ of revelation;" the object of faith is "the whole word of God, explicit and implicit, as dispensed by His living Church;"[36] and after 1870 he could tell the Duke of Norfolk and Mr Gladstone that dogmatic definitions, deliberately rare though they be, are "the word of the Church as God's oracle."[37] The climax may come in the 1877 preface to the third edition of the *Lectures on the Prophetical Office of the Church*: "When our Lord went up on high, He left His representative behind Him. This was Holy Church, His mystical Body and Bride, a Divine Institution, and the shrine and organ of the Paraclete, who speaks through her till the end comes."[38]

Put those together — "the ark of salvation," "the embodiment of Christianity," "the organ of revelation," "God's oracle," "the Body and Bride of Christ," "a Divine Institution," "the shrine and organ of the Paraclete" — and you are close to Karl Rahner's designation of the Church as the "Grundsakrament." Without quite calling the Church such a "basic sacrament," Newman specifies the "sacramentality" of the Church in various points. "From the Sacramental principle come," wrote Newman in the *Essay on the Development of Doctrine*, not only "the Sacraments properly so

---

[35] *Diff.*, i: 368-369.

[36] Letters of March 22 and 23, 1867 to E. B. Pusey, in *LD*, xxiii: 99, 105.

[37] *Diff.*, ii: 320.

[38] *VM*, i: xxxix. The paragraph continues with a typically dialectical move: "She, to use an Anglican poet's words, is 'His very self below,' as far as men on earth are equal to the discharge and fulfilment of high offices, which primarily and supremely are His."

called," but also "the unity of the Church, and the Holy See as its type and centre" (not to mention "the authority of Councils; the sanctity of rites; the veneration of holy places, shrines, images, vessels, furniture, and vestments").[39] In connection with the sacramentality of the Church, three kinds of questions continue to arise also in contemporary ecumenism: whether there is salvation outside the Roman Catholic Church; how the unity of the Church is to be conceived and "reintegrated;" and what is the proper role of the Petrine office that the see of Rome claims to hold.

First, salvation inside and outside the Roman Catholic Church. As he struggled towards his own conversion, Newman had been troubled by a fear lest he or his friends die outside the Church of Rome;[40] we have already heard from the Brompton lectures of 1850 the concern of Newman the convert for the souls of his former co-religionists; and there is the extraordinary record from 1878 of Newman's desire to persuade E. B. Pusey on his putative deathbed of the "right" of "the Catholic Roman Church" to "claim him as her child."[41] Retrospectively, Newman could say of his own case, that "God's mercy did for me, what the system I was in did not."[42] In May 1843 he had already written to Keble that he "consider[ed] the Roman Catholic Communion the Church of the Apostles, and that what grace is among us ... is extraordinary, and from the overflowings of [God's] Dispensation."[43] As a Roman Catholic, Newman could speak of "proceedings and works among Protestants which it is but Christian charity to

---

[39] *Essay on the Development of Doctrine*, 94.

[40] See Ker, *John Henry Newman*, 286, 289, 297.

[41] Letter of March 31, 1878 to H. P. Liddon, in *LD*, xxviii: 337.

[42] Letter of November 5, 1862 to "Mr Richard Pope's friend," in *LD*, xx: 340.

[43] Letter of May 4, 1843 to John Keble, cited by Ker, *John Henry Newman*, 274-275.

ascribe to the influence of divine grace."[44] The Church of England was merely "a human work and a political institution," whose members might as individuals be saved "by a superabundant mercy of God which He has not promised and covenanted."[45] Others than Roman Catholics might, thought Newman in the *Letter to the Duke of Norfolk*, "belong to the soul of the Church without belonging to the body."[46] At 5.30 a.m. on the very day when he would in the evening be received into the Roman Catholic Church, Newman had written to his sister Jemima of his continuing firm belief that "individuals in the English Church are invisibly knit into that True Body of which they are not outwardly members."[47]

Now Protestants are not too keen on being consigned to the uncovenanted mercies of God or having their invisible ecclesiality somehow mediated by the Roman Catholic Church.[48] Since the Roman Catholic Church's own entry into the twentieth-century ecumenical movement, its theologians have in fact had to struggle towards an account of the evidences of Christianity outside its institutional bounds. The Vatican II decree on ecumenism spoke of those Christians who by faith and baptism are put "in some, though imperfect, communion with the Catholic Church" and, taking a further step, declared that their "churches and communities,"

---

[44] Letter of September 18, 1864 to Ambrose Phillipps de Lisle, in *LD*, xxi: 228.

[45] Letter of September 16, 1873 to Miss Rowe, in *LD*, xxvi: 364. There was no more grace to be received from the Church of England, "though she had a dozen sacraments instead of two," than "an infant could receive nourishment from the breast of its dead mother" — so Newman in a letter of December 20, 1881 to Mrs Lydia Rose Christie, in *LD*, xxx: 34.

[46] *Diff.*, ii: 335.

[47] Letter of October 9, 1845 to Mrs John Mozley, in *LD*, xi: 14.

[48] On the "inconsistency" of the notion of uncovenanted mercies, see Lesslie Newbigin, *The Household of God* (London: SCM Press, 1953) 78-79.

despite their defects, are "not without meaning and importance in the mystery of salvation" — "for the Spirit of Christ has not refrained from using them as means of salvation which derive their efficacy from the very fulness of grace and truth entrusted to the Catholic Church."[49] The question of ecclesiality between Roman Catholics and Protestants is, of course, a mutual one; and a complementary move to that made in *Unitatis Redintegratio* is reflected on the part of the Methodists, for example, in the 1991 report on "The Apostolic Tradition" from the Joint Commission between the Roman Catholic Church and the World Methodist Council: "Catholic and Methodist formularies differ over the concrete location of the Church which they both confess. While Wesley and the early Methodists could recognize the presence of the Christian faith in the lives of individual Roman Catholics, it is only more recently that Methodists have become more willing to recognize the Roman Catholic Church as an institution for the divine good of its members;" and the text goes on, from the Catholic side, to apply the terms of the Vatican II decree on ecumenism to Methodists and to Methodism. The challenge addressed by Catholic ecclesiology to ecumenical Protestants is that they should not remain content with a view of ecclesial unity as simply the aggregate of existing denominations.

From discussion of the unicity of the Church we have slid into discussion of its unity, and that is natural, for, as *Dominus Iesus* insisted, the two are intimately connected. In his Anglo-Catholic days, Newman had held that the unity of the Church was, let us say, "impaired," to the detriment of the Church's various "branches." According to the New Testament, he showed in the *Lectures on the Prophetical Office of the Church* of 1837, "the promises made to [the Christian Church] did depend more or less

---

[49] *Unitatis Redintegratio*, 3.

upon a condition which now for many centuries she has broken. This condition is Unity, which is made by Christ and His Apostles, as it were, the sacramental channel through which all the gifts of the Spirit, and among them purity of doctrine, are secured to the Church."[50] With the shift in perspective brought by his conversion to the Roman Catholic Church as the one true Church, Newman could see "the Blessed Sacrament, ready for the worshipper even before he enters" the building, as the sign, and perhaps the instrument, of existing ecclesial unity as he now understood it: "There is nothing," he wrote from Milan on his way to Rome in October 1846, "which has brought home to me so much the Unity of the Church, as the presence of its Divine Founder and Life wherever I go — All places are, as it were, one."[51] In the ecumenical movement today, judgment is still required as to the relationship between the eucharist's functions as a sign of existing unity and as an instrument towards the increase and deepening of unity. Much depends on the dynamic viewed as appropriate to the reintegration of ecclesial unity. In Vatican II's decree on ecumenism, the implied picture was of the dispersed elements of Christianity being drawn back to the Catholic Church, like filings magnetically returning to the original block. In his ecumenical encyclical *Ut Unum Sint* of 1995, however, Pope John Paul II could say that "the Church of Christ is effectively present," albeit imperfectly, in "other Christian communities;" and even the generally more reticent *Dominus Iesus* could speak of "the Church of Christ" as "present and operative" at least in other "Churches"

---

[50] *VM*, i: 199. "The want of unity has injured both them and us," Newman wrote to Keble; and perhaps it was "unity," he wrote to Robert Wilberforce, which would bring holiness to both Churches rather than the other way round (letters of 29 December 1844 and 26 January 1842 respectively, cited by Ker, *John Henry Newman*, 244).

[51] Letter of October 4, 1846 to Mrs J. W. Bowden, in *LD*, xi: 254.

that are properly so called.[52] It seems to me that the category of "operative presence" affords the best hope of a recognition by the Roman Church of the ecclesiality of others without abandonment of its own fundamental self-understanding, while encouraging the others towards a more genuinely organic understanding of what complete unity requires.

That the latter calls for some kind of Petrine office has come to be more widely perceived in the last two decades of the twentieth century. In his Anglo-Catholic days Newman could admit of the Roman see that such "a center of unity may have been intended for the Church in process of time," without its being "infallible."[53] As a Roman Catholic, Newman saw the Pope's ministry as "to bind the whole of Christendom into one polity;" and he further saw that this entailed universal jurisdiction: "An honorary head, call him primate or premier duke, does not affect the real force, or enter into the essence of a political body, and is not worth contending about. We do not want a man of straw, but a bond of unity."[54] Newman held that, in the circumstances of his time, an attempt to reach agreement on the papacy would be like building "St. Peter's from the cross and ball;" rather, "we must begin from the bottom

---

[52] *Ut Unum Sint*, 10-14; *Dominus Iesus*, 17.

[53] "Fall of De La Mennais," *Essays Critical and Historical*, I: 150, 172; cf. the letter of November 25, 1840 to F. Rogers, in *Moz.*, ii: 285: "It is quite consistent to say that I think Rome the *centre* of unity, and yet not to say that she is infallible, when she is by herself."

[54] Letter of March 23, 1867 to E. B. Pusey, in *LD*, xxiii: 106. Of the four Anglican responses that regretted the failure of *Baptism, Eucharist and Ministry* to take up the question of a Petrine ministry, three came from churches that took the lead in developments within Anglicanism that run counter to current positions of the see of Rome: the Episcopal Church in the USA was the first to ordain women to the diaconate, to the presbyterate, and to the episcopate; the Church of the Province of New Zealand elected the first woman diocesan bishop; and at the Lambeth Conference of 1998 the primus of the Scottish Episcopal Church was the most outspoken advocate of homosexual causes.

— not even only from the foundations of the building, but from the soil in which the foundations must be placed."[55] In our time, we made in our Methodist-Catholic dialogue a first approach to the question of the papacy in our 1986 report, "Towards a Statement on the Church" and did indeed perceive that we needed to dig deeper, and so subsequent reports were devoted to the more fundamental questions: "The Word of Life: A Statement on Revelation and Faith," "The Apostolic Tradition," and "Speaking the Truth in Love: Teaching Authority among Catholics and Methodists."[56] Meanwhile, Pope John Paul II himself, noting "the ecumenical aspirations of the majority of the Christian Communities," has invited their leaders and theologians to a "patient and fraternal dialogue" as he seeks "a way of exercising the primacy which, while in no way renouncing what is essential to its mission, is nevertheless open to a new situation."[57] I have myself put forward the "respectful suggestion" that "the Pope should invite those Christian communities which he regards as being in real, if imperfect, communion with the Roman Catholic Church to appoint representatives to cooperate with him and his appointees in formulating a statement expressive of the Gospel to be preached to the world today. Thus the theme of the 'fraternal dialogue' which John Paul II envisaged would shift from the *theory* of the pastoral and doctrinal office to the *substance* of what is believed and preached. And the very *exercise* of elaborating a statement of faith might — by the very process of its launching, its execution, its resultant form, its publication, and its reception — illuminate the

[55] Letter of December 15, 1869 to J. P. Taylor, in *LD*, xxiv: 391.

[56] Apart from their official publication by the World Methodist Council and by the Pontifical Council for Promoting Christian Unity (in its *Information Service*), the international Roman Catholic-Methodist reports appear in a number of theological journals, most consistently in *One in Christ*.

[57] *Ut Unum Sint*, 88-97.

question of 'a ministry that presides in truth and love'. *Solvitur ambulando.*"[58]

As a final remark on the sacramental nature of ecclesial unity, I may perhaps be allowed to note at least one meeting of minds between Newman and Wesley. On learning that his republished *Parochial and Plain Sermons* were selling well even among Nonconformists, the Catholic Newman recognized that different "ecclesiastical principles" did not preclude the sharing of "ethical and religious sentiments;" indeed he judged that "the first step towards unity was a unison of feeling," as a "necessary foundation, on which higher strata of truth might be deposited at some future day."[59] For "whatever tends to create a unity of heart between men of separate communions, lays the ground for advances towards a restoration of that visible unity, the absence of which among Christians is so great a triumph and so great an advantage to the enemies of the Cross."[60] A century and a quarter earlier, John Wesley had preached his sermon on "Catholic Spirit" and penned his "Letter to a Roman Catholic," in which he had urged that, while present differences prevented "an entire external union," yet they should not stop "a union in affection;" and, given the consensus in the cardinal points of the faith, Christians of the different communions should "help each other on in whatever we are agreed leads to the Kingdom."[61] What Wesley and Newman in their respective ways desired, we have now had placed closer to our reach.

[58] Geoffrey Wainwright, "'The Gift Which He on One Bestows, We All Delight to Prove': A Possible Methodist Approach to a Ministry of Primacy in the Circulation of Truth and Love," *Petrine Ministry and the Unity of the Church*, ed. James P. Puglisi (Collegeville, MN: Liturgical Press, 1999) 59-82, in particular, 82.

[59] Letter of November 26, 1868 to W. J. Copeland, in *LD*, xxiv: 177.

[60] Letter of January 28, 1868 to the Revd Henry Allon, in *LD*, xxiv: 22.

[61] Sermon 39, "Catholic Spirit," *Works of John Wesley*, Bicentennial Edition, volume 2, ed. A. C. Outler (Nashville, TN: Abingdon Press, 1985), in particular,

The Word of God Incarnate

From the Church as "Grundsakrament" we may now, in Karl Rahner's terminology, move to the primordial Christ himself as "Ursakrament." That way of putting things began perhaps with Henri de Lubac: that "Christ is the Sacrament of God" is the assumption behind the statement that "the Church is for us the Sacrament of Christ."[62] But the movement of thought has a biblical grounding in the Church as the Body of Christ, who is himself the Word made flesh, the Mystery of God now present in human history.

John Henry Newman had a very robust sense of Jesus Christ as the God-Man. Listen to Newman preaching in his Oxford days on "The Tears of Christ at the Grave of Lazarus":

> It is very much the fashion at present to regard the Saviour of the world in an irreverent and unreal way — as a mere idea or vision; to speak of Him so narrowly and unfruitfully, as if we only knew of His name; though Scripture has set Him before us in His actual sojourn on earth, in His gestures, words, and deeds, in order that we

82; "Letter to a Roman Catholic," *Works of John Wesley*, ed. T. Jackson (London: Wesleyan Conference Office, [3]1872), volume X, in particular, 85-86.

[62] Henri de Lubac, *Catholicisme* (Paris: Cerf, 1947) 50: "Si le Christ est le Sacrement de Dieu, l'Église est pour nous le Sacrement du Christ." For various applications of the category "sacrament" to Christ, the Church, and the world in Catholic theology, see my "Sacramental Theology and the World Church," *Proceedings of the Catholic Theological Society of America* 39 (1984) 69-83. The Oxford Anglican theologian Oliver Quick almost got there in *The Christian Sacraments* (London: Nisbet, 1927). Given a christology more "Antiochene" than "Alexandrian," Quick's formulations make the human reference of sacrament somewhat more prominent than the divine: "As Jesus Christ Himself is the perfect sacrament of created being, so in the light of that one sacrament the Church appears as the sacrament of human society, Baptism as the sacrament of man's spiritual birth to God, Holy Communion as the sacrament of human fellowship in Him, holy days as sacraments of time, and holy places as sacraments of space" (106).

may have that on which to fix our eyes. And till we learn to do this, to leave off vague statements about His love, His willingness to receive the sinner, His imparting repentance and spiritual aid, and the like, and view Him in His particular and actual works set before us in Scripture, surely we have not derived from the Gospels that very benefit which they are intended to convey.... When we contemplate Christ as manifested in the Gospels, the Christ who exists therein, external to our own imaginings, and who is as really a living being, and sojourned on earth as truly as any of us, then we shall at length believe in Him with a conviction, a confidence, and an entireness, which can no more be annihilated than the belief in our senses. It is impossible for a Christian mind to meditate on the Gospels, without feeling, beyond all manner of doubt, that He who is the subject of them is God; but it is very possible to speak in a vague way of His love towards us, and to use the name of Christ, yet not at all to realize that He is the Living Son of the Father, or to have any anchor for our faith within us, so as to be fortified against the risk of future defection.[63]

Newman continued to maintain that position as a Roman Catholic, saying in his review of Seeley's *History* that "what Catholics ... have ever lived on ... is the Christ Himself, as He is represented in concrete existence in the Gospels;" and He it is who is now believed in as "a Presence in the sacred Tabernacle, not as a form of words, or as a notion, but as an Object as real as we are real."[64] After his worries in his final years as an Anglican concerning "the inward evidence of the Presence of Christ with us in the Sacraments" — worries that he recognized might be regarded as "a sort of methodistic self-contemplation"[65] — Newman the newly

---

[63] *PS*, iii: 130-131. Much later, Newman would attribute the declension of French and Italian Catholics from the Christian faith to the fact that "they have not impressed upon their hearts the life of our Lord and Saviour as given us in the Evangelists" — so a letter of May 12, 1872 to Mrs J. W. Bowden, in *LD*, xxvi: 87.

[64] "An Internal Argument for Christianity," *Discussions and Arguments on Various Subjects*, 388.

converted Roman Catholic found great comfort at the Maryvale house. Writing from next door to the chapel where the Sacrament was reserved, Newman told Henry Wilberforce: "It is such an incomprehensible blessing to have Christ in bodily presence in one's house, within one's walls, as swallows up all other privileges and destroys, or should destroy, every pain. To know that He is close by — to be able again and again through the day to go in to Him;" and to Mrs J. W. Bowden: "I could not have fancied the extreme, ineffable comfort of being in the same house with Him who cured the sick and taught His disciples, as we read of Him in the Gospels, in the days of His flesh."[66] From Milan in September 1846 he wrote that his preference for the "Grecian" or "Italian" style of church architecture over the "Gothic" rested on its "open countenance," with the Altar "so gracious and winning, standing out for all to see": "Nothing moves there but the distant glimmering Lamp which betokens the Presence of our Undying Life, hidden but ever working."[67] In Newman's novel *Loss and Gain*, Charles Reding's impending conversion appears clinched by what he witnesses at Catholic worship: "A cloud of incense was rising on high; the people suddenly all bowed low; what could it mean? The truth flashed on him, fearfully yet sweetly; it was the Blessed Sacrament — it was the Lord Incarnate who was on the altar, who had come to visit and to bless His people. It was the Great Presence, which makes a Catholic Church different from every other place in the world; which makes it, as no other place can be, holy."[68]

---

[65] *Apologia*, ed. Martin Svaglic, 145.

[66] Letters of February 26, 1846 to Henry Wilberforce, and of March 1, 1846 to Mrs J. W. Bowden, in *LD*, xi: 129 and 131 respectively.

[67] Letters of September 24, 1846 to W. G. Penny and to Henry Wilberforce, in *LD*, xi: 249 and 252 respectively.

[68] *LG*, 427. When, at the time of the First Vatican Council, rumours circulated that Newman might be returning to the Church of England, he wrote that he would

The sense of Christ's presence and saving work is memorably captured when Newman writes to Catherine Froude that the Blessed Sacrament, the sacraments and sacramentals all convey that "the Atonement of Christ is not a thing at a distance, or like the sun standing over against us and separated off from us, but that we are now surrounded by an *atmosphere* and are in a medium, through which His warmth and light flow in upon us on every side."[69]

Whatever the private opinions of individual theologians, there are no dogmatic differences between the Catholic Church and the classic Protestant churches in christology; and there have been strong indications in recent decades that the differences between the Chalcedonian and the "pre-Chalcedonian" churches are being resolved.

In official ecumenism over the second half of the twentieth century, helped by the spread of the Liturgical Movement, there was gained, in principle, a good sense of the complementarity between word and sacrament as vehicles of Christ's presence and work. That is well illustrated by the responses of the churches to the Faith and Order statement, *Baptism, Eucharist and Ministry*.[70] Nevertheless, differences remain, as we have noted, over the relation between Christ's presence and the bread and wine; and some of those differences recur over the connected, though not identical, question of the eucharistic remains and their reservation.

be "the most asinine, as well as the most ungrateful of men, if I left that Gracious Lord who manifests Himself in the Catholic Church, for those wearisome Protestant shadows, out of which of His mercy He has delivered me" — so a letter of August 23, 1870 to H. T. Ellacombe, in *LD*, xxv: 195.

[69] Letter of June 16, 1848 to Mrs William Froude, in *LD*, xii: 224.

[70] See Geoffrey Wainwright, "From Word and/or Sacrament to 'Verbum Caro' = 'Mysterium Fidei': Lessons Learned from the 'BEM' Process," *Parola e Sacramento*, ed. Patrick Lyons (Roma: Pontificio Ateneo S. Anselmo, 1997) 141-175.

The responses to *BEM* allowed no advance over what the original document itself had said:

> The way in which the elements are treated requires special attention. Regarding the practice of reserving the elements, each church should respect the practices and piety of the others. Given the diversity in practice among the churches and at the same time taking note of the present situation in the convergence process, it is worthwhile to suggest:
> – that, on the one hand, it be remembered, especially in sermons and instruction, that the primary intention of reserving the elements is their distribution among the sick and those who are absent, and
> – on the other hand, it be recognized that the best way of showing respect for the elements served in the eucharistic celebration is by their consumption, without excluding their use for communion of the sick.[71]

The Sacraments Properly So Called

As a way in, at last, to "the sacraments properly so called," a few indications must be given of Newman's perception of the relations between persons, words, deeds, and things, particularly as these impact his understanding of the sacraments.[72] Sacramental theologians familiar with linguistic analysis and communication theory will hear intimations of what are now labelled "performative language," "speech-acts," and so on.

In the *Lectures on Justification* of 1838, there is a key passage in which Newman shows from Scripture that the Word of God "has a sacramental power, being the instrument as well as the sign of His will":

---

[71] *Baptism, Eucharist and Ministry*, E 32 (16-17).

[72] The larger topic is, of course, Newman's epistemology, and a proper treatment would require attention to the *Grammar of Assent*, but the following will at least provide some hints on the semiotical side.

God's word, I say, effects what it announces. This is its characteristic all through Scripture. He "calleth those things which be not, as though they are," and they are forthwith. Thus in the beginning He *said*, "Let there be light, and there *was* light." Word and deed went together in creation; and so again "in the regeneration, *"The Lord gave the word*, great was the company of the preachers." So again in His miracles, He *called* Lazarus from the grave, and the dead arose; He *said*, "Be thou cleansed," and the leprosy departed; He *rebuked* the wind and the waves, and they were still; He *commanded* the evil spirits, and they fled away; He said to St. Peter and St. Andrew, "Follow Me," and they arose, for "His word was with power;" and so again in the Sacraments His word is the consecrating principle. As He "blessed" the loaves and fishes, and they multiplied, so He "blessed and brake," and the bread became His Body.[73]

Newman's main argument was to demonstrate that "justification is an announcement or fiat of Almighty God, which breaks upon the gloom of our natural state as the Creative Word upon Chaos; and that it *declares* the soul righteous, and in that declaration, on the one hand, conveys *pardon* for its past sins, and on the other *makes* it actually *righteous*."[74] Baptism appears as "the token of God's election," the one "ordained method on earth for the absolute pardon of sin," the "channel" or "cause" of regeneration; it "was called of old the Sacrament of faith, as being, on the part of the recipient, only an expression by act of what in words would be 'I believe and I come'" — for "faith is inculcated in the outward sign [of the Sacraments], and required for their inward grace; and is as little disparaged by the Catholic doctrine concerning them, as Christ Himself by the doctrine of faith."[75]

Human words have reality only when they deal authentically or "consistently" (a favourite expression of Newman's) with things.

[73] *Jfc*, 81.

[74] *Ibid.*, 83.

[75] *Ibid.*, 323, 320, 318, 321, 287, 288 respectively.

There is another passage in the *Lectures on Justification* which makes that point while also conveying what today might be designated a "holistic" view of man in his relation to God:

When I assign an office to faith, I am not speaking of an abstraction or creation of the mind, but of something existing. I wish to deal with things, not with words. I do not look to be put off with a name or a shadow. I would treat of faith as it is actually found in the soul; and I say it is as little an isolated grace, as a man is a picture. It has a depth, a breadth, and a thickness; it has an inward life which is something over and above itself; it has a heart, and blood, and pulses, and nerves, though not upon the surface.... Love and fear, and heavenly-mindedness, and obedience, and firmness, and zeal, and humility, are as certainly one with justifying faith, considered as a thing existing, as bones, muscles, and vital organs, are necessary to that outward frame of man which meets the eye, though they do not meet it.[76]

Newman puts the encounter between God and humankind graphically thus: "In a Christian [ordinance], God speaks the word, and man kneels down and is saved."[77] More systematically, he concludes this part of his controversy with the "Lutheran" view of justification thus: "It seems, then, that whereas Faith on our part fitly corresponds, or is the correlative, as it is called, to grace on God's part, Sacraments are but the manifestation of grace, and good works are but the manifestation of faith; so that, whether we say we are justified by faith, or by works, or by Sacraments, all these but mean this one doctrine, that we are justified by grace, which is given through Sacraments, impetrated by faith, manifested in works."[78]

---

[76] *Ibid.*, 265.

[77] *Ibid.*, 287-288.

[78] *Ibid.*, 303. The concreteness of the human encounter with God is strikingly illustrated in a curious passage from 1863, in which Newman undertakes to justify a theologically erroneous devotional practice when it is performed by an ardent but usually undemonstrative English Catholic whereas it is reprehensible in the

None of this is meant to undo the dialectical relation between Revelation and Mystery, about which Newman early wrote thus:

> It may seem a contradiction to call Revelation a Mystery; but is not the book of the Revelation of St. John as great a Mystery from beginning to end as the most abstruse doctrine the mind ever imagined? Yet it is called a Revelation.... A Revelation is religious doctrine viewed on its illuminated side; a Mystery is the selfsame doctrine viewed on the side unilluminated. Thus Religious Truth is neither light nor darkness, but both together; it is like the dim view of a country seen in the twilight, with forms half extricated from the darkness, with broken lines, and isolated masses. Revelation, in this way of considering it, is not a revealed *system*, but consists of a number of detached and incomplete truths belonging to a vast system unrevealed, of doctrines and injunctions mysteriously connected together; that is, connected by unknown media, and bearing upon unknown portions of the system.... What was hidden altogether before Christ came, could not be a mystery; it became a Mystery, then for the first time, by being disclosed at His coming.... [With reference to 1 Timothy 3:16,] the great secret has, by being revealed, only got so far as to be a Mystery, nothing more; nor could become a Manifestation (that is, a system comprehended as such by the human mind), without ceasing to be anything great at all. It must ever be small and superficial, viewed only as received by man; and is vast only when considered as that external truth into which each Christian may grow continually, and ever find fresh food for his soul.[79]

case of superficial Italians: "In England Catholics pray *before* images, not *to* them. I wonder whether as many as a dozen pray *to* them, but *they* will be the *best* Catholics, not ordinary ones. The truth is, that sort of affectionate fervour which leads one to confuse an object with its representative, is skin-deep in the South and argues nothing for a worshipper's faith, hope and charity, whereas in a Northern race like ours, with whom ardent devotion feeling is not common, it may be the mark of great spirituality" — thus a letter of October 25, 1863 to W. R. Brownlow, in *LD*, xx: 544.

[79] "On the Introduction of Rationalistic Principles into Revealed Religion" *Ess.*, i: 41-44. "System" is a favourite word of Newman's, and he uses it in many contexts, some sublime, some trivial. The overall effect on reading him is to

In this context Newman goes on to speak of "the chief doctrines of the Gospel Revelation":

> the Holy Trinity; the Incarnation of the Eternal Son; His Atonement and merits; the Church as His medium and instrument through which He is converting and teaching mankind; the Sacraments, and Sacramentals (as Bishop Taylor calls them), as the definite channels through which His merits are applied to individuals; Regeneration, the Communion of the Saints, the Resurrection of the body, consequent upon the administration of them; and lastly, our faith and works, as a condition of the availableness and efficacy of these divine appointments. Each of these doctrines is a Mystery.... Thus the Atonement: — *why* it was necessary, *how* it operates, is a Mystery; that is, the heavenly truth which is revealed, extends on each side of it into an unknown world. We see but the skirts of God's glory in it. The virtue of the Holy Communion; how it conveys to us the body and blood of the Incarnate Son crucified, and how by partaking it body and soul are made spiritual. The Communion of Saints; in what sense they are knit together into one body, of which Christ is the head. Good works; how they, and how prayers again, influence our eternal destiny.[80]

In his review of Milman's *History of Christianity*, Newman applied the already cited "one great rule on which the Divine Dispensations with mankind have been and are conducted" as the "animating principle" of "the Church's ritual": this "sacramental" principle "makes the ceremonies and observances to be signs, seals, means, and pledges of supernatural grace."[81] The Sacraments, he had told Samuel Wilberforce in 1835, are "embodied forms of the Spirit of

strengthen the impression he leaves of organic connectedness, such as marks so profoundly the *Essay on the Development of Doctrine*, or of analogical relationships among the many works of God, such as we found him retaining from Joseph Butler.

    [80] "On the Introduction of Rationalistic Principles into Revealed Religion," *Ess.*, i: 45-46.

    [81] *Ess.*, ii: 192-193.

Christ," though as an Anglican Newman felt bound to lament that "our fault at this day is, that the very *name* of them does not kindle us."[82] Newman blamed the Reformation for the "modern," "unscriptural system, which promising liberty conspires against it; which abolishes Christian sacraments to introduce barren and dead ordinances; and for the real participation of the Son, and justification through the Spirit, would, at the very marriage feast, feed us on shells and husks, who hunger and thirst after righteousness."[83] Seeing "the sacramental system" as "better secured in Rome than in the Anglican Church" was, he tells us in the *Apologia*, a factor in his conversion.[84]

Humanly spoken words and humanly performed gestures gain sacramental power when they are spoken and performed in the divinely appointed context and way. "He who made the creature, gives it its uses... It is superstitious to ascribe power to the creature where God has not given it; and profane to deny it where He has."[85] The Sacraments are "sensible tokens of God's favour" — for "religion is of a personal nature, and implies the acknowledgment of a particular Providence, of a God speaking, not merely to the world at large, but to this person or that, to me and not to another."[86]

What, concretely, are these Sacraments, according to Newman? In *Tract 90* Newman allowed, and indeed affirmed, the distinction made in Anglican Article XXV between the two "Sacraments of the Gospel" and "those five commonly called Sacraments." "Baptism and the Lord's Supper" were clearly and directly "ordained by Christ" and are "generally necessary to salvation;"

---

[82] Letter of March 10, 1835 to Samuel Wilberforce, in *LD*, v: 39.
[83] *Jcf.*, 57.
[84] *Apo.*, 113.
[85] *Jcf.*, 317-318.
[86] *Ibid.*, 323.

but "Confirmation, Penance, Orders, Matrimony, and Extreme Unction" could — in the "wider" rather than the "stricter" sense — be called sacraments as "outward sign[s] of an invisible grace," falling within the Church's "power of dispensing grace through rites of its own appointing," since the Church "is endowed with the gift of blessing and hallowing the 'rites or ceremonies' which, according to the twentieth article, it 'hath power to decree'." Newman went on to quote from his own *Lectures on Justification* a passage that states relations among most of the septenary that he would need only to nuance slightly as a Roman Catholic:

> The Roman Catholic considers that there are seven [sacraments]; we do not strictly determine the number. We define the word generally to be an "outward sign of an inward grace," without saying to how many ordinances this applies. However, what we do determine is, that CHRIST has ordained two special sacraments, as *generally necessary to salvation*. This, then, is the characteristic mark of those two, separating them from all other whatever; and this is nothing else but saying in other words that they are the only *justifying* rites, or instruments of communicating the Atonement, which is the one thing necessary to us. Ordination, for instance, gives *power*, yet without making the soul *acceptable* to God; Confirmation gives *light and strength*, yet is the mere *completion* of Baptism; and Absolution may be viewed as a negative ordinance removing the *barrier* which sin has raised between us and that grace, which by inheritance is ours. But the two sacraments "of the Gospel," as they may be emphatically styled, are the instruments of inward *life*, according to our Lord's declaration, that Baptism is a new *birth*, and that in the Eucharist we eat the *living* bread.[87]

The Roman Catholic nuance is supplied in a footnote to the 1874 edition of the *Lectures on Justification*:

> Catholics hold that there are two justifying Sacraments, in the sense in which the word "justification" is mainly used in this volume

[87] "Remarks on Certain Passages of the Thirty-Nine Articles," *VM*, ii: 310-314.

— that is, sacraments which reconcile the sinner to God, or *sacramenta mòrtuorum* — viz. Baptism and Penance. The other five are *sacramenta vivorum*, that is, they presuppose the subject of them to be in a state of grace, or justified, and increase his justification. To regard the Holy Eucharist as justifying, in the same light as that in which Baptism justifies, is to confuse the first justification of the sinner with the farther justification of the already just.[88]

By the second half of the twentieth century much Roman Catholic sacramental theology was ready to embrace the idea of baptism and the eucharist as what Yves Congar in a celebrated article called the two "sacrements majeurs ou principaux" — a move of ecumenical significance.[89] And in relation to Newman's other nuance, the *Joint Declaration on the Doctrine of Justification*, ratified in 1999 between the Roman Catholic Church and the Lutheran World Federation, surely has even wider and deeper ecumenical potential.

What, finally, of the liturgical order, ritual performance, and pastoral practice of the particular sacraments as we find them in Newman? At St. Mary's in Oxford he refused in 1834 to conduct the marriage of an unbaptized woman of Baptist parenthood because he "considered the unbaptized to be outcast from Christian privileges and blessings."[90] At Littlemore he installed "a font large enough for immersion" — at least in the case of children.[91] As a Roman Catholic he became unused to pastoral duties, and once in Birmingham he worried about the validity of a baptism he had had to perform: "The water was exhausted out of the

---

[88] *Jcf.*, 153-154.

[89] Yves M. J. Congar, "The Notion of 'Major' or 'Principal' Sacraments," *The Sacraments in General*, ed. E. Schillebeeckx and B. Willems, *Concilium* 31 (New York: Paulist Press, 1968) 21-32.

[90] Letter of July 10, 1834 to the Editor of the Oxford Conservative Journal, in *LD*, iv: 299. For the whole episode, see Ker, *John Henry Newman*, 103-104.

[91] Letter of August 23, 1836 to W. Dodsworth, in *LD*, v: 342.

abominable shell before I made the three crosses — and I made a hash of it."[92]

As Vicar of St. Mary's Newman introduced a weekly Communion service, early on Sunday mornings, although even at the time (he said later) he had found the actual liturgy "clumsy and dreary," leaving him with "an extreme distaste and dislike" of Anglican services.[93] Already in 1836, in a letter to Hugh James Rose, he confided that the Prayer Book "alterations in the Eucharistic Service seem to me a *sin* — not in us but in our forefathers. It is our *misfortune* — and I bear it resignedly, as I should the loss of a limb;" with regard to the prayer of consecration in particular, Newman bemoaned "the evanescent state of the *prosphora*, the omission of the Prayer to the Holy Ghost."[94] Poor practice with the consecrated remains belied, according to Newman, a belief in the Real Presence and added a further argument against Anglican orders.[95] Newman was not ashamed, however, to cite lay communion *sub una* as an example of "the development of doctrine": "And for some wise purpose doubtless, such as that of showing the power of the Church in the dispensation of divine grace, as well as the perfection and spirituality of the Eucharistic Presence, the Chalice is in the West withheld from all but the celebrant in the Holy Eucharist."[96]

The twentieth-century Liturgical Movement, ecumenical in scope, has confirmed some of Newman's insights and corrected

[92] Letter of June 13, 1858 to Ambrose St. John, in *LD*, xviii: 378.

[93] See Ker, *John Henry Newman*, 103, 194, 200, 356, 510.

[94] Letter of May 23, 1836 to H. J. Rose, in *LD*, v: 304-305. Newman considered the Anglican eucharistic rite as "mortally wounded" at the Reformation, and it could "no more have life breathed into it again, than a corpse by galvinism be revivified" — so a letter to an unknown correspondent, in *LD*, xxviii: 216.

[95] Letter of July 30, 1857 to Ambrose Lisle Phillipps, in *LD*, xxviii: 104; letter of August 5, 1868 to Fr Henry James Coleridge, in *LD*, xxiv: 116.

[96] *Essay on the Development of Doctrine*, 380.

some of the abuses which he either lamented or winked at. *Baptism, Eucharist and Ministry* favours immersion and the ample use of water.[97] Baptism and Confirmation are viewed as parts of "a unitary and comprehensive process" of Christian initiation.[98] Word and Table is now widely regarded, in principle and sometimes in practice, as the normal pattern for the main service on the Lord's Day. The recovery of the eucharistic anaphora along West Syrian lines has introduced an epiclesis of the Spirit into the liturgies of many denominations (indeed Prayers II, III, and IV of the Roman Missal of 1969 now have two of them!). Catholic laypeople may now receive from the Cup. Good ecumenical practice, as we have noted, now requires careful attention to the consecrated remains.

A Higher Gift Than Grace?

As a Methodist I may perhaps be allowed to conclude with a hymn. In his broadest sacramental vein, John Henry Newman speculated that "musical sounds and their combinations" might be the "momentary opening and closing of the Veil which hangs between the worlds of spirit and sense," perhaps even "some reflexion, as in an earthly mirror, of some greater truths above."[99] From Newman's *Dream of Gerontius* the hymnals of many denominations have taken "Praise to the Holiest in the height." The British *Methodist Hymn Book* of 1933 — on which I was raised — wittingly or unwittingly retained the reference to created grace in the fourth stanza, whereas some other hymnals — such as *The Hymnal 1982* of the Episcopal Church in the USA — bowdlerized

---

[97] *Baptism, Eucharist and Ministry*, B 18 (6-7).

[98] *Baptism, Eucharist and Ministry 1982-1990: Report on the Process and Responses* (Geneva: World Council of Churches, 1990) 112.

[99] Letter of November 4, 1860 to Miss Mary Holmes, in *LD*, xix: 415.

the first line of that verse, so as to give "grace" here the sense, right enough in itself, of God's favour; thus:

> And that the highest gift of grace
> Should flesh and blood refine ...

On any reckoning the hymn pays powerful tribute to the God-Man, "Christus, Sacrament van de Godsontmoeting" (as Edward Schillebeeckx called him), Jesus Christ who is in his Person and Work the primary and permanent Sacrament:

> Praise to the Holiest in the Height
> And in the depth be praise:
> In all His words most wonderful;
> Most sure in all His ways.
>
> O loving wisdom of our God!
> When all was sin and shame,
> A second Adam to the fight
> And to the rescue came.
>
> O wisest love! that flesh and blood
> Which did in Adam fail,
> Should strive afresh against the foe,
> Should strive and should prevail;
>
> And that a higher gift than grace
> Should flesh and blood refine,
> God's Presence and His very Self,
> And essence all divine.
>
> O generous love! that He who smote
> In man for man the foe,
> The double agony in man
> For man should undergo;
>
> And in the garden secretly,
> And on the cross on high,
> Should teach His brethren and inspire
> To suffer and to die.

And congregational singing repeats the first stanza:

> Praise to the Holiest in the Height
> And in the depth be praise:
> In all His words most wonderful;
> Most sure in all His ways.[100]

---

[100] From "The Dream of Gerontius," in *VV*, 363-364.

NEWMAN THROUGH THE LOOKING GLASS

Elizabeth JAY

For a man notably lacking in vanity in matters of personal appearance Newman was remarkably drawn to looking in mirrors. Two of the *Apologia's* most famous passages recall this habit. First, the passage recalling his work in the Long Vacation of 1839 on the Early Church when doubts as to the Via Media first crossed his mind:

> My stronghold was Antiquity; now here, in the middle of the fifth century, I found, as it seemed to me, Christendom of the sixteenth and the nineteenth centuries reflected. I saw my face in that mirror, and I was a Monophysite.[1]

And second, the great jeremiad upon "the dreary hopeless irreligion" of the human race:

> The world seems simply to give the lie to that great truth, of which my whole being is so full; and the effect upon me is, in consequence, as a matter of necessity, as confusing as if it denied that I am in existence myself. If I looked into a mirror, and did not see my face, I should have the sort of feeling which actually comes upon me, when I look into this living busy world, and see no reflexion of its Creator.[2]

What is striking about both these images is not merely the self-reflexivity of a man who had famously declared a youthful distrust of material phenomena so strong that it made him rest "in the thought of two and two only absolute and luminously self-evident

[1] *Apo.*, 108.
[2] *Ibid..*, 216.

beings, myself and my Creator,"[3] but the "vision to dizzy and
appal"[4] that lurks behind these mirrors — "so fearfully yet exactly
described in the Apostle's words, 'having no hope and without God
in the world'." The underlying anxiety has less to do with the theological conviction that the human race as a whole has repudiated
and departed from the image in which it was made, than with a
more sharply personal fear that if the evidence of the material world
and of history itself were to be accepted, then the two poles of
Newman's existence would collapse, leaving him without recognisable identity: "I should be an atheist, or a pantheist, or a poly-
theist."[5] *The Dream of Gerontius* represents death as the supreme
expression of this fear:

> Tis this strange innermost abandonment,....
> This emptying out of each constituent
> And natural force, by which I come to be. (ll. 9-12)
> That sense of ruin, which is worse than pain,
> That masterful negation and collapse
> Of all that makes me man; as though I bent
> Over the dizzy brink
> Of some sheer infinite descent... (ll. 109-113).

At the point when the body itself fails to offer material evidence
of identity: — "I cannot make my fingers or lips/By mutual pressure witness each to each" (ll. 204-205) — Gerontius is rescued
from the nightmare of dissolution by God's grasp:

> ...'tis not a grasp
> Such as they use on earth, but all around
> Over the surface of my subtle being,
> As though I were a sphere, and capable
> To be accosted thus, a uniform

[3] *Ibid.*, 18.
[4] *Ibid.*, 217.
[5] *Ibid.*, 216.

And gentle pressure tells me I am not
Self-moving, but borne forward on my way.[6]

Those who have teased out the threads of Newman's utterances upon conscience, conversion and belief have often commented upon the inherent circularity of Newman's belief system.[7] Circular arguments operate a kind of "belt and braces" approach to logic, ensuring the desired conclusion by embedding it in the premise — creating as it were a defensive enclosure against any imagined attack. In Newman's case circular argument maintained the required imaginary distance necessary to separate the believer and the object of belief against the implosion that would ultimately threaten belief, believer and the objective existence of the Supreme Being. With a mind that had been exposed to the pervasive whiff of Oriel Common Room logic, Newman could not but be aware of this problem. The jeremiad in the *Apologia*, to which I have already referred, begins in this way:

> Starting then with the being of a God, (which, as I have said, is as certain to me as the certainty of my own existence, though when I try to put the grounds of that certainty into logical shape I find a difficulty in doing so in mood and figure to my satisfaction,) I look out of myself into the world of men, and there I see a sight which fills me with unspeakable distress.[8]

The passage ends, many, many parallel sub-clauses and phrases later, with an appeal beyond logic: the dizzying vision "inflicts upon the mind the sense of a profound mystery, which is absolutely beyond human solution." The choice of the word "inflicts," more often

---

[6] *The Dream of Gerontius and Other Poems* (London: Oxford University Press, 1914).

[7] See particularly, Cyril Barrett, "Newman and Wittgenstein on the Rationality of Religious Belief," *Newman and Conversion*, ed. Ian Ker (Edinburgh: T.&T. Clark, 1997) 89-99.

[8] *Apo.*, 216.

associated with *wounding* blows, rather than a more conventional word, such as "impresses," to describe the impact upon the mind of "profound mystery," offers its own commentary upon the embattled nature of Newman's consuming preoccupation with the relation between faith and reason. In the case of a writer as merciless as Newman could be with his opponents' casual choice of words, it is not unreasonable to examine his own style for the sophisticated strategies he deployed as defender of the faith. The inventive accumulation and variation of parallel phrases, separating the beginning from the end of so many of Newman's sentences, for instance, suggest something of the mental agility and nervous energy required to keep subject and object apart. The virtuoso displays of Newman's syntax are often deployed, like his circular arguments, to sustain that illusion of distance or ground gained between the point of departure and the conclusion, between the Creator and his creation, so necessary to Newman's sense of his own coherent identity.[9]

[9] For those with a penchant for Lacanian analysis, the ways in which Newman approaches matters of faith and reason might be reformulated as follows. Lacanian theory is predicated upon the impossibility of a whole or unifed personality. Infants develop an imaginary identity, known as the "mirror stage" of development, in which they attain a false, narcissistic sense of wholeness of being by locating this "Ideal-I" in the fixed, inverted symmetry of "the image in the mirror," or in the intimately satisfying, presence of the mother, both of which seem so different from the turbulent movements that the subject feels are [inwardly] animating him'. Hence the "self" is envisaged as a "mental permanence" at the same time as it is prefigured as other: "a statue in which man projects himself" and in which "the world of his own making tends to find completion" (Jacques Lacan, "The Mirror Stage," trans. A. Sheridan. reprinted in *Literary Theory: An Anthology*, ed. Julie Rivkin and Michael Ryan [Oxford: Blackwell, 1998] 178-183) In Lacan's, exclusively male-oriented, theory, once this relationship is ruptured by the social taboo which proclaims the mother an inappropriate object of completion and desire, the child enters into the Symbolic order where language functions as metaphor, always trying to describe by substitution, by naming as Other, that imagined unifying presence. Newman's habit of treating both friends and books as a succession of mirrors in which "the world of his own making" could find a

The *Apologia pro Vita Sua*, is everywhere marked, as Owen Chadwick has convincingly shown, by this need to resist the imputation of inconsistency, and demonstrate to himself and others "the unity of Newman's personality... and of a course, which looked to the outer eye to be divided into two contradictory parts."[10] The way in which Newman achieves this illusion of consistency and a unified personality is partly, as Chadwick observes, by using his former Anglican friends and Protestant influences as building blocks incorporated in the final Catholic construction, which admitted of no further change. It is a habit of which Newman indeed convicts himself in Chapter 2 of the *Apologia*: "I wished men to agree with me, and I walked with them step by step, as far as they would go; this I did sincerely; but if they would stop, I did not much care about it, but walked on."[11] "Moving on" is of course another pervasive motif in Newman's rhetorical repertoire. It is there, as many critics have remarked, as much in the 1833 poem, "Lead, kindly light," as in his notion of "development," or in the "journey" each Christian soul must make. Yet, as many mid-nineteenth century critics of the notion of "progress" were busy pointing out, it was all too easy to read purposive movement into aimless bustle and transition.[12]

---

satisfying completion, until he discovered a way of conceiving a personal relation with the Christian God which would guarantee him "being," "history," a "present condition," and a "future... which no one else could share" appears to conform to the process, identified by Lacan, of using language within the Symbolic Order to come to terms with lack of being through using a substitute signifier. In the Christian faith system, of course, God satisfies human desire for impossible completion by being both absolutely present and absolutely Other.

[10] Owen Chadwick, "A Consideration of Newman's Apologia pro Vita Sua," *Newman From Oxford to the People: Reconsidering Newman and the Oxford Movement* , ed. P. Vaiss (Leominster:Gracewing, 1996) 163-185.

[11] *Apo.*, 51.

[12] Chapter 19 of Dickens's novel *Bleak House*(1852), entitled "Moving On," employs the phrase to point up the way in which the realities of vagrancy can be

In Newman's deliberately teleological application this vocabulary of movement is again intended to establish the distance
between himself and the still-point of the God whose absolute existence guarantees the ground of his being. Even more satisfyingly,
from Newman's point of view, the vocabulary of movement could
be yoked to circular argument to achieve the effect of a revolution
of the wheel gained, thus justifying the pain of the labour taken to
arrive at the beginning "and know the place for the first time."[13]
The terrifying night-time scramble "O'er moor and fen, o'er crag
and torrent," in "The Pillar of the Cloud" will prove "with the
morn" to have been part of a divine plan when "those angel faces
smile/Which I have loved long since, and lost awhile."[14] Whether
we read these "angel faces" with Sheridan Gilley, as the same
angel faces Newman had glimpsed as a child in the gardens of Grey
Court, Ham,[15] or whether we see in them an example of the Pla-
tonist affinity Newman shared with the Romantic poets, detected
by David Newsome,[16] the "moving on" which returns us back to
a "sure" point remains the same. "So long Thy power hath blest
me; sure it still/Will lead me on" begins the final verse of "The Pillar of the Cloud." Pivotally balanced between the first and second
clause, the adjective "sure" can be attached backwards to apply to
God as "certain, or reliable," or forwards, in the sense "secure, or
tranquilly confident," as applied to the one who is being led on.
In God's unchangeability lay the guarantee of the coherence of

deliberately occluded by officialdom's use of the term to suggest progress to
another destination.

[13] T. S. Eliot, "Little Gidding," *The Four Quartets* (London: Faber and
Faber,1942) l. 242.

[14] "The Pillar of the Cloud" (1833), *The Dream and Other Poems*, 141.

[15] Sheridan Gilley, *Newman and His Age* (London: Darton, Longman and
Todd, 1990) 9.

[16] David Newsome, "Coleridge and Newman," *Two Classes of Men:
Platonism and English Romantic Thought* (London: John Murray, 1974) 57-72.

Newman's unified personality, the integrity of his pilgrimage from Evangelicalism to Roman Catholicism and his uninterrupted "happiness" in the decision he had reached in becoming a Catholic. In a recent account of the *Apologia* Owen Chadwick identified the word *"securus"* as a key motif of the book's discursive practice and drew particular attention to the passage where, at the start of Chapter V, "Position of My Mind since 1845," Newman speaks of the safe haven he has reached and begins: "From the time that I became a Catholic, of course I have no further history of my religious opinions to narrate."[17] Chadwick agrees that this reads oddly, not to say ironically, to a modern reader, but explains that Newman's sense of safety here is bound up in his relief at no longer having to rely upon his own "opinions."[18]

Part of the problem, for the modern reader, however, lies in that word "opinions," to which the *Apologia* returns again and again. "Opinion" in today's parlance, has been largely devalued to indicate that something is "a matter of opinion," that it is capable of sustaining mutually incompatible, subjectively-determined interpretations. (Law courts invite "expert opinion" but the evidence of such witnesses is not necessarily conclusive). Newman's use of the word "opinion," appears to slide between several different usages: between denoting "a judgement reached, a definitely-held belief about an item of one's religious or political creed," which, when applied to the tenets of a theological system like Calvinism, becomes practically identical with "conviction," [OED] and the notion of "a pious belief,... opinion, or... conjecture"[19] about which it might be proper, if it seemed sufficiently probable, to have a "certitude." It was Bishop Butler's *Analogy* (1736), which

---

[17] *Apo.*, 214.
[18] Chadwick, "A Consideration of Newman's Apologia pro Vita Sua," 180.
[19] *Apo.*, 31.

focussed Newman's attention on this concept.[20] The discussion in the *Apologia* of Butler's teaching on "probability" was not the rather arid logical exercise it is inclined to seem today, but of central importance to Newman because it ultimately had to do with "Private Judgement in religion, that is, of a Private Judgement, not formed arbitrarily and according to one's fancy or liking, but conscientiously, and under a sense of duty." And here was the nub of the problem for Newman: Bishop Butler's *Analogy* had employed the word "opinion" in a way that made it clear that it could apply to "a belief in something as probable, or as seeming to *one's own mind* (my italics) to be true" (*OED*) when that belief might turn out to be inimical to religion and morality. As early as April 1823 Newman had been exercised by the life-and-death implications of this doctrine: he wrote to his brother, Charles:

> We find one man of one opinion in religion, another of another; and thus may be led hastily to conclude that opinions diametrically opposite to each other may be held without danger to one side or the other in a future state; but contradictions can be no more true in religion, than in astronomy or chemistry — and there is this most important distinction, to those who believe in revelation, between scientific and religious opinions, that, whereas errors in the former are unattended with danger to the person who maintains them, he who holdeth not "the faith" (I am not now determining what that faith is), such a one is said to be incapable of true moral excellence, and so exposed to the displeasure of God.[21]

Eventually, as we know, for Newman, the tradition of the Catholic Church provided his haven of interpretative authority,

---

[20] See Joseph Butler, *The Analogy of Religion, Natural and Revealed, to the Constitution and course of nature*, Part One, ch. 6: "Of the Opinion of Necessity, considered as influencing practice." For the importance of Butler in Newman's intellectual formation, see Newsome, "Coleridge and Newman," 73-76.

[21] J. H. N. to C. R. Newman, 12 Dec. 1823. *The Letters and Diaries of John Henry Newman*, ed. Charles Stephen Dessain, *et al.*, vols. i-vi (Oxford: Clarendon

supplying both "the whole revealed dogma as taught by the Apostles," and "those new dogmatic definitions which are from time to time made, and which in all times are the clothing and the illustration of the Catholic dogma as already defined."[22]

What interests me, however, is why "Private Judgement" and its attendant spiritual ills became so important a focus in his journey from Anglicanism to Roman Catholicism. The traditional explanation has been that Newman's investment in the Evangelical religion of his early life had, on reflection, led him to distrust the concept of "justifying faith" as one which inevitably returned men to the examination of self rather than to contemplating the awful mystery of God. But, in Newman's Tractarian writings, the phrases he uses to deplore the solipsistic tendency of the Evangelical creed often become curiously intertwined with the vocabulary and arguments he deploys to expose the soul-deadening iniquities of "Rationalism." Indeed his 1839 article on "The State of Religious Parties"[23] laid the blame if not fairly, at least squarely, at the door of Evangelicalism for sowing "the seeds of ruin" by "sanctifying" Private Judgement in a way that would ensure that some of its devotees would soon embrace "avowed liberalism." The link between the two positions and the very real threat that they posed to Newman becomes even clearer in his 1836 Tract 73, "The Rationalistic and the Catholic Spirit Compared" where he writes,

> Our private judgement is made everything to us, — is contemplated, recognised, and referred to as the arbiter of all questions, and as independent of everything external to us. Nothing is considered except so far forth as our minds discern it.

Press, 1978-1984); vols. viii-ix (Oxford: Clarendon Press, 1995-1999); vols. xi-xxii (London: Nelson, 1961-1972); vols. xxiii-xxxi (Oxford:Clarendon Press, 1973-1977), i: 169-170.

  [22] *Apo.*, 224-225.
  [23] *The British Critic* (April 1839) 418-419.

That last sentence, "Nothing is considered except so far forth as our minds discern it" provides the key, I would argue, to the very personal nature of the threat that Newman detected in Rationalism. In its claim to be able to deduce God from the evidence provided in His Creation, the rationalist tradition of eighteenth-century deism enjoyed a materialist basis that seems totally inimical to the anti-materialist bias of the young Newman's cast of mind, but both processes brings us to an alarmingly similar position: in each case we are returned to the preoccupations of a solitary mind, which could veer shockingly, for little apparent reason other than innate temperament, to the opposite poles of secular rationalism or an inherently circular belief system.

By the mid-1830s Newman had good reason to reach this conclusion. His profound scepticism about the place of the intellect in faith went well beyond the proper spiritual humility about intellectual achievement that a devout young Anglican priest serving in Oxford would have done well to cultivate. It was not that Newman ranked the gift of intellect low in the spectrum of God-given abilities. He never, for instance, seems to have entertained the notion that he had a duty to abandon his mission to the educated classes in favour of an exclusive ministry to the poor and needy. Nor did he doubt his own intellectual abilities. Rather, it was a far more deep-seated anxiety about the part played by the mind in matters of faith that surfaced in the particular slant of his contribution to the Tractarian project. The reasons for this were close to home.

John Henry Newman and his brother Francis William (Frank) had enjoyed a similar upbringing, education, and to the outward eye at least, religious trajectory, until early manhood. It is not my purpose to retrace the changing contours of a fraternal relationship which was to end in the two occupying opposing corners in the nineteenth-century fight between faith and rational scepticism: this was done at length in William Robbins, *The Newman Brothers: an*

Essay in Comparative Intellectual Biography.[24] Sufficient to remark that by 1826, an *"unhealable"* breach had arisen between the two on matters of religious belief.[25] John could not attribute this theological divergence to Frank's intellectual inferiority, for, in 1826, Frank had taken a double first, whereas John, six years earlier, had achieved only a third and a pass. Nor was he likely to attribute Frank's divergence of opinion to mere whimsicality. Both John and Frank were now very aware that they would have to rely upon their own efforts to make their way in the world, and the necessity Frank faced, of surrendering his Balliol fellowship when he found himself unable to sign the Thirty-Nine Articles again, was no light matter. Instead, it appears, from a letter of Frank's, that John, doubting his younger brother's "health and spirits" ascribed his behaviour to "melancholy."

> Your fears both for my health & spirits are... groundless... never in my life [have I had] so stable a peace, at times such real joy... it is nothing in my *religion* that makes me melancholy: but the prevalence of *sin* grievously wounded me. I sought to the cross, & I was eased: I thought that I was pardoned: — But presently I was again lulled in carelessness & fell into *wilful* sin; & then where was my peace!... I cannot at all express the anguish of mind, the despair into which I have often fallen for my horrible iniquity... I just say enough to magnify Jesus, who, I trust, saves me amid much weakness; and to show you that if I spoke strongly of my mental trouble, I had indeed ample cause.[26]

Melancholy is one of those portmanteau words that in the early nineteenth-century covered a wide spectrum of mental conditions. Like "nervous weakness" it could imply anything from edgy tetch-

---

[24] William Robbins, *The Newman Brothers: An Essay in Comparative Intellectual Biography* (London: Heinemann, 1966).

[25] Francis William Newman, *Contributions Chiefly to the Early History of the Late Cardinal Newman* (London:Kegan Paul, Trench, Trübner & Co., ²1891) vi.

[26] F. W. N. to J. H. N., 1826, quoted in Robbins, *The Newman Brothers,* 27.

iness to the existence of deep neuroses. The connection between mind and body was at best conjectural and so defining psychiatric disorder was an uncertain business, often heavily reliant upon cultural assumptions. The rule of thumb belief in *mens sana in corpore sano* meant that cause and effect could be argued either way: nervous disorders might emanate from organic causes, or they could be held to be the result of violent emotions or passionately-embraced ideas. Healthy attitudes as well as physique were considered essential to mental well-being. Morality could thus be linked into the chain as an issue of health. Reason was contingent upon the operation of the will which exerted a supervisory function over the "lower" impulses. Madness ensued when the will lost the ability to regulate thoughts and feelings.[27] John's anxious inquiry as to Frank's "health & spirits" should not therefore be simply translated as John arrogantly assuming that anyone who chose to disagree with him must be mad, but a query concerned with the perplexing relation between the intellect, the body, and matters of belief and morality. Frank and he were blood relations who had grown up under remarkably similar influences. If, as academic examination had so recently proved, there was ostensibly nothing wrong with Frank's intellectual equipment, it would have been reasonable for an early nineteenth-century mind to inquire if there was some physical cause, and, if this was so, might it not turn out to be an inherited weakness that might surface elsewhere in the family?

The Newman boys' father, who, by his sons' accounts, was of a very different temperament from them, felt he had reason to be anxious on their account. When John had backed Frank against his father, back in 1822, in a row about Sabbath observance, John senior had written:

---

[27] Janet Oppenheim, *"Shattered Nerves:" Doctors, Patients, and Depression in Victorian England* (New York and Oxford: Oxford University Press, 1991) 41-43.

Take care, It is very proper to quote Scripture, but you poured out texts in such quantities. Have a guard. You are encouraging a nervousness and morbid sensibility, and irritability, which may be very serious. I know what it is myself, perfectly well. I know it is a disease of mind. Religion when carried too far, induces a softness of mind... Do nothing ultra.[28]

By 1835 John, believing Frank to be "in great peril" from his belief that "everyone may gain the true doctrines of the gospel for himself from the Bible," felt that until he could be brought to abandon this conviction "there is no hope for a clear-headed man like you. You will unravel the web of self-sufficient inquiry."

> You will tell me perhaps that you must pursue truth without looking to consequences — yet I cannot help begging you to contemplate whither you are going. Is it possible that you are approaching Charles's? [sic] notions.

He hastened to assure Frank he was not really imputing to him their middle brother, Charles's, Owenite Socialism and disbelief: "There will be this difference that you will admit the being of God', — a fairly substantial theological difference one would have thought."[29] So why bring their middle brother into the argument? As early as 1823 Charles had so shocked his senior in a discussion, lasting from Turnham Green to Knightsbridge, that John Henry felt impelled to make a record of the rationalist tone of his brother's remarks.[30] In 1830 John Henry reported,

> My head, hands and heart all knocked up with the long composition I have sent Charles. I have sent him twenty-four closely-written foolscap pages all about nothing. He revived the controversy

---

[28] Entry for 6 Jan. 1822, *Letters and Diaries*, i: 117.

[29] J. H. N. to F. W. N., 23 Nov. 1835, *Letters and Diaries*, v: 166.

[30] J. H. N.: *Autobiographical Writings*, ed. Henry Tristram (London and New York: Sheed & Ward, 1956) 192.

we had five years ago. I have sent him what is equal to nine sermons.[31]

Charles's career had already shown signs of the temperamental and
mental instability that were twice to lead the Newman family to take
an opinion on his sanity.[32] In the two preceding years he had resigned
his post at the Bank of England, run through his maternal inheritance,
lost a job as a school usher as a consequence of having bitten a boy
and quarrelled with the Principal, and moved in with a woman who
promptly locked him up and pawned his clothes to support her drinking habit.[33] For the final twenty-five years of his life he was cared for
as a reclusive eccentric in Tenby. A letter of 1862 from John Henry
to the local Protestant parson in Tenby, thanking him for the kindness to Charles he has already shown and urging him to attempt to
awaken in Charles a "true belief and acceptance of our Lord as his
only Saviour" reveals how far beyond the possibility of receiving
instruction Newman believed his brother Charles had now slipped:

> Of course, as a Catholic, I could wish him to believe, not only this
> candid truth, but to be guided into *all* the truth,… but, when a soul
> has not that means of learning more, it is a comfort for friends to
> know that in "repentance towards God and faith in our Lord Jesus
> Christ," all other truths and acts of religion are included.[34]

---

[31] *Letters and Correspondence of John Henry Newman during His Life in the
English Church*, ed. Anne Mozley, 2 vols. (London: Longmans, Green & Co.,
1898) i: 205.

[32] J. H. Newman wrote that "at times he has seemed to his friends to be mad
actually; indeed, he has at time so called himself… though twice in 1834[?] and
1845, when a medical judgment was taken on the point, it was to the effect that
no restraint could legally be put on his liberty" ("Memorandum on Charles
Newman, May 1874," *Letters and Diaries*, i: 182).

[33] Gilley, *Newman and His Age*, 56 supplements the account given by Frank
of Charles's "very eccentric character" in *Contributions Chiefly to the Early History of the Late Cardinal Newman*, vii-viii.

[34] J. H. N. to Rev. G. Clark, 16 March 1862, *Letters and Diaries*, xx: 172.

And yet, as Newman reflected in 1874, Charles had initially exhibited "more than ordinary abilities," displaying a "turn for philosophical research" and a capacity for languages (he had spent three years in Bonn in the 1840s, though he had left without taking a degree). Unfortunately, John Henry reflected, all this had been marred by the way he breaks "out into acts of wildness and cruelty, chiefly towards his relations, into mad acts as a relief to himself of the irritation, the fierce indignation he has felt at his own distressing impotence of mind."[35]

In pursuing the trace of "melancholy" or "nervousness and morbid sensibility, and irritability," that some at least of the Newman family believed themselves heir to, — Charles's own opinion was that "all the Newmans are mad," only Frank being madder than John Henry[36] — I am not arguing that we should discount Newman's theology because he suffered from "hereditary insanity" or a genetic disposition to insanity. Rather I am drawing attention to the particular cast given to his theology by the ever-present fear that the intellect might be unhinged at any time by somatic disorder or moral impairment, a fear for which, to his own way of thinking, his kith and kin provided ample evidence. Indeed the Victorian belief that a childhood tendency to daydreaming and night terrors, both of which Newman lays claim to in the opening paragraphs of the *Apologia*, might be seen as the premonitory symptoms of nervous disorder in later life,[37] possibly intensified Newman's fear of succumbing to mental instability. In the *Apologia* the risks associated with the intellect are often spoken of in ways which, for the

---

[35] "Memorandum," *Letters and Diaries*, i: 182. John and Frank agreed that in his seclusion in Tenby Charles had become gentle and calm and won the affection of those who cared for him.

[36] "Memorandum," *Letters and Diaries*, i: 182, supplemented by Gilley, *Newman and His Age*, 56.

[37] Oppenheim, *"Shattered Nerves"*, 235.

mass of humanity, we might feel to be luridly overstated: Newman writes of the "suicidal excesses" of which the unrestrained intellect is capable and of the fitness of infallible teaching for "smiting hard and throwing back the immense energy of the aggressive, capricious, untrustworthy intellect."[38] Looking back over the events of his life Newman might have identified that week in the winter of 1820 when he had "utterly broken down"[39] in his final examinations at Oxford, or the delirious fever that struck him down in Sicily in the summer of 1833, as instances of the folly of relying upon the intellect for temporal, yet alone eternal, salvation. On occasion Newman gave voice to doubts about his own mental condition: in 1852, overwhelmed by the deaths in swift succession of his sister Harriet and his beloved aunt Elizabeth, by mounting legal bills, the trials of a tour of Ireland, and the threat of impending imprisonment he wrote that the specialist, Sir Benjamin Brodie, had told him "that unless I got out of anxiety and let my nerves rest, I should die Swift's death."[40]

Not long afterwards, in the long vacation of 1855, Newman resumed work on his novel *Callista: A Sketch of the Third Century*. In a postscript to the novel, added when his authorship of this anonymously published work had got abroad, Newman explained that he had written the "great part of Chapters I., IV., and V., and sketched the character and fortunes of Juba, in the early spring of 1848."[41] Fundamental to Newman's conception of this novel, then, was a character with a supernumerary plot function (Juba's part in saving Bishop Cyprian could easily have been left to another character). Newman created Juba for two inter-related reasons: first, he

[38] *Apo.*, 220.
[39] *AW*, 47.
[40] J. H. N. to John Joseph Gordon, 20 Nov. 1852, *Letters and Diaries*, xv: 199-120.
[41] *Call.*, vii-viii.

manifests insanity in a variety of forms and second, this man whose intellectual arrogance, we are required to believe, makes him an easy prey to insanity, is cast as the younger brother of Agellius, the novel's putative hero.

Perhaps a brief plot summary, foregrounding Juba's part, may be in order here. The two brothers, Agellius and Juba, are respectively eight and seven when their father, Strabo, a former Roman legionary, dies. Strabo had settled in Sicca in North Africa, taken a wife, and converted, late in life, to Christianity. Discovering "that the Church did not oblige him to continue or renew" his marital vows to a spouse whose malignant profligacy had won her the popular reputation of communing with evil spirits, he had separated from her and left his young sons to the care of their uncle, Jucundus, a successful trader in heathen statues and amulets. By the time of their father's death the older brother, Agellius, had been baptised, confirmed and become a communicant, but Juba remains a catechumen.

> [N]othing would make him go forward in his profession of Christianity, no earthly power would be able to make him go back. So there he was, like a mule, stuck fast in the door of the Church, and feeling a gratification in his independence of mind.[42]

A year also separated John Henry Newman from his next brother, Charles Robert, and it had been an argument about the efficacy of baptism which had been the first dogmatic stumbling-block to John's relationship with Frank.

Stranded in Sicca by the work he has found as a farm under-bailiff, Agellius maintains his faith but is deprived of the nourishing support of a thriving church, the wave of Christianity having long retreated from the shores of North Africa. The similarities to the position John Henry felt himself to have been living under in the recent times, as

---

[42] *Ibid.*, 22.

he looked back in the spring of 1848 when he began the novel, are not hard to identify. His parents were both dead, and even Jemima, the only one of his siblings from whom he was not estranged, had now forbidden him her house. His reception into the Catholic Church would also have reconfigured Newman's mental cartography: from a position at the heart of a Protestant empire he had now become a marginal figure in an outpost of a Catholic empire whose centre was Rome. Agellius's lonely vigil and prayers in a simply furnished rustic cottage, reminiscent of Newman's sojourn at Littlemore and subsequently at Maryvale, are subject to disrupting visits from his brother, Juba, who glorying in the sense of "being his own master," and therefore capable of sampling without succumbing to any religious experience on offer, taunts Agellius for being too careful of his reputation to suffer the indignities consequent upon open declaration of his Christianity. Juba displays the traits of Charles and Francis Newman in an odd amalgam. He has all Charles's obstinacy, eccentricity, selfishness and anti-religious stance, combined with Francis's intellectual scepticism. In 1846 Francis had been made professor of Latin at University College, London, a secular foundation where he could practise his conviction that education should be kept free from religion. That summer John wrote of a visit from Frank in tones recalling Agellius's resentment at being disturbed by Juba:

> My brother is coming to see me at Maryvale. I saw him yesterday. [[Why should he come?]] I think he has some obscure idea he can decide whether there are thumb-screws and the like at Maryvale.[43]
> *Agellius*: You began in coming in here; what in the world are you come for? by what right do you disturb me at this hour?
> There was no appearance of anger in Juba; he seemed as free from feeling of every kind, from what is called heart, as if he had been a stone.[44]

[43] J. H. N. to Ambrose St. John, 11 July, 1846, *Letters and Diaries*, xi: 204.
[44] *Call.*, 32.

John Henry Newman had long been encouraged by his mother to picture himself as "such a sensitive being" and Frank as "a piece of adamant."[45] Juba disappears into the night, singing the scurrilous Satanic snatch that becomes his signature tune. For ten chapters Juba lies low while the main business of the novel is advanced. He reappears when his brother, Agellius, is being nursed back to health from a fever. Newman who was accustomed to interpreting his own serious illnesses as psychological turning points, intimates that Agellius's fever springs partly from the trauma of his rejection by the Greek girl, Callista, who tells him that he is capable of teaching her nothing of the Christian God to whom she feels so strangely attracted and partly from fear of the new wave of Christian martyrdom advancing upon Sicca. When Juba reappears at Agellius's country cottage, again no plot purpose is furthered. Rather he is summoned to the reader's presence, as a marker of Agellius's spiritual progress. Agellius is being cared for, physically and spiritually, by a Christian priest in disguise, who subsequently turns out to be Cyprian, Bishop of Carthage. At the very point when Cyprian assures Agellius that by becoming "simply the instrument of Another" "he will save his own soul and others," Juba turns up to boast that he rejoices in the "dignity" of being a "free man."[46] The priest sees in Juba "pride in bodily shape, treading down faith and conviction," while Juba, resenting the priest's threat to his independence of mind and soul, claims that he can suppress the voice of conscience within him. The priest, nevertheless, prophesies that those marked as Christ's sheep will not escape the fold however strong their "irrational aversion to home." Five chapters later Juba again reappears, this time at the head of a drunken city mob out to sate themselves with the blood of a Christian. Juba's purpose in

[45] Mrs J. Newman to J. H. N., 13 June, 1826, *Letters and Diaries*, i: 291.
[46] *Call.*, 162-163.

partaking in this heathen revel, it transpires, is to free Cyprian, thus proving to his own satisfaction that morality, or the capacity to "forgive and forget" is not a Christian prerogative.[47] Juba's identification with the mob, combined with his desire to demonstrate morality as a stronger humanitarian imperative than dogma, recalls Frank's support for the Chartist cause during the hungry forties and the ethical programme outlined in *his Catholic Union: Essays Towards a Church of the Future* (1844).

The next time we see Juba he has gone to visit his mother, the witch, Gurtha, who, despite the African setting, is close kin to the witches in Macbeth. The relish she displays for persecuting Christians and for her bloodthirsty sacrifices of children turns the stomach of even her son Juba, who refuses to swear his allegiance to her satanic master any more than to the Christian God. Enraged by her favourite son's refusal to take the devil's part, Gurtha bewitches him, providing him with a familiar who pursues him in his frenzied flight through the forest, uttering, as if from the depths of his own being, the words, "You cannot escape from yourself."[48] Juba is seized by a terror so strong that he faints — the first of many swoons that perhaps indicate epilepsy. In the following chapter Gurtha's curse is worked through: in a series of extraordinary scenes Juba tears apart the wild animals of the jungle with his bare hands, gorging himself on their flesh and drinking their blood, but at dawn stands, like Milton's Satan overlooking paradise, forced, against his will, to recognise the peace and sweetness of creation's witness against him. Juba's punishment for asserting independence of mind and will is total enslavement: lashed by the Furies he dances in Bacchic mode, speaks in tongues and, like some grotesque Puck, disrupts village feasts. Finally he reaches his

---

[47] *Ibid.*, 231.
[48] *Ibid.*, 265.

uncle's house in Sicca where he ejects his brother Agellius from his newfound place of safety and lies down to sleep in the bed from which he has ousted him. The emphasis in this act of substitution upon the brothers' potential interchangeability is reinforced by the strong hint that Juba is also attracted to the Greek girl, Callista. Juba, having served his turn as fraternal double, is hustled offstage again for the next few chapters, before he is found wandering the mountains, in self-mutilating madness, a living witness to the limits of the self-determining will. Bishop Cyprian tames him with the sign of the cross and leads him to the safety of the caves where the remnants of the Christians of Carthage have fled. There he is entrusted to a man whose task it is to care for the *energumens* or devil-possessed. Though calmed by the ministrations of exorcists his demonic possession is only finally routed by the miraculous effects of the holy body of Callista, restored to its former beauty from the ravages of her martyrdom, and preserved as a relic in the caves. When his demon departs Juba falls to the ground, apparently lifeless, and, when he comes to, quietly joins the other worshippers at mass; "he was quite changed: he was quiet, harmless, and silent; the evil spirit had gone out; but he was an idiot."[49] For ten years he merely exists, unable even to learn "to sweep the sacred pavement" until one night Callista appears to him in a dream, restoring his sanity, and he approaches the bishop for baptism. Left praying by St. Callista's tomb he dies that very night, still in his baptismal robe. In the ensuing and last paragraph of the novel Agellius's martyred body is placed with Callista's and by implication he is reunited with his brother.

Juba's madness derives, as I have indicated, from a mélange of the Gospel accounts of demonic possession, classical mythology, and tales of witchcraft and folklore, while the dramatic seizures, to

[49] *Ibid.*, 381.

which his possession leaves him vulnerable, mimic the symptoms of epilepsy. Both the causes and symptoms of his madness flirt with but never finally embrace an explanation based upon heredity. Juba's involuntary craving for blood echoes his mother's condition, but the familiar with which she endows him suggests that he is a victim of her witchcraft rather than her genes. His quasi-epileptic fainting fits are also ambiguous in origin. Until the eighteenth-century epileptic fits were commonly interpreted as the result of demonic possession, but nineteenth-century diagnosis had begun to perceive links with conditions such as morbid introspection and to see affinities between the onset of epilepsy and that sense of incorporeality, so vividly described at the opening of the Apologia:[50] "I thought life might be a dream, or I an Angel, and all this world a deception."[51]

At one level the tale of Juba is easy to interpret: he exists as a dramatic signifier of Newman's distrust of "the immense energy of the aggressive, capricious, untrustworthy intellect." Juba's much-vaunted independence of mind is unable to withstand the onslaught of his mother's witchcraft; but this moral could easily have been painted without making Juba bloodbrother to Agellius. Bloodbrother he may be, but temperamentally these two brothers are about as different as it is possible to conceive: the one as naturally disposed to faith as the other is to proclaim rationalism. The fraternal relation, nurtured in a constant family environment, is naturally disposed to form a good laboratory for contemplating the divergent personality types that can emerge from the same gene pool, and, in the case of the Newman brothers, the extreme dissimilarity of John, Charles and Frank's mental cast was to become, I believe, the basis for John Henry's lifelong interest in the features that distinguished the believing from the non-believing mind,

---

[50] *Apo.*, 16.
[51] Oppenheim, *"Shattered Nerves"*, 81.

and to lead him to minimize the part reason played in arriving at faith. If the ratiocinative powers that Charles and Frank, in their different ways, relied upon so heavily could so easily be betrayed by either demonic manipulation or hereditary frailty, it was as well to place belief and the object of belief beyond the realm of pure logic and anchor it in a subjective response to a personally apprehended God. Identifying a capacity for logic as their shared inheritance and then cordoning it off as both potentially treacherous and, in matters of faith, useful only to the devout mind, provided John Henry with a safety barrier against the twin threats of infidelity and madness.

Newman's fiction has often been read as a vehicle for self-representation. Charles Reding's journey from Anglicanism to Roman Catholicism in *Loss and Gain* (1847) could not but invite readers to look for the traces of its author's recent experiences. *Callista* too, despite its exotic historical setting, has been subject, from its earliest reviews, to autobiographical interpretation,[52] but the analogical emphasis has fallen upon Callista, and, to a lesser extent, Agellius. The novel's central plot allowed Newman "to feminize," or render harmless, the intellect in the person of the educated Greek girl, Callista, who repudiates the philosophy of her fellow Greeks because it "dwelt only in conjecture and opinion," in favour of an "instinctive notion of religion [as] the soul's response to a God who had taken notice of the soul."[53] Callista rehearses Newman's circular proof of identity when she discovers in her personal relation with the Christian God "her being, her history, her present condition, her future... which no one else could share with her."[54]

[52] *Christian Remembrancer*, 33 (Jan. 1857) 135.
[53] *Call.*, 293.
[54] *Ibid.*, 328.

Callista's intellectual and spiritual pilgrimage towards Christian martyrdom, also repeats the pattern of examining fraternal relationship. Her only brother, Aristo, the closest family bond she has ever known, invokes philosophy and legal logic-chopping to rescue his sister, but at the end the classical values he represents are fatally undermined when we see him stop short of the noble suicide he has planned. The need to recognise the Christianity practised by the Early Fathers as a faith superior to familial, cultural and racial forces inevitably played an important part in a novel designed to demonstrate the claims of Roman Catholicism to nineteenth-century English readers. For all the long-drawn out process of Callista's conversion and the carefully documented stages of her physical martyrdom, Callista is putty in Newman's hands: an essentially passive character who, apart from her much advertised feminine beauty, inhabits Newman's mental and emotional world with ease, never showing any instability of purpose on the path to her ultimate destination.

When we transfer the focus to Juba, however, the marginal character whose character and fortunes were the first part of the novel to be mapped, we begin to see ways in which the mirror of fiction allowed Newman to reflect upon, and simultaneously deflect, more worrying aspects of his own fragmented personality. Recent theorising on the relation between writing and madness has tended to think of writing about madness as a means of controlling, subjugating and expelling it. "To talk about madness" claims the French psychoanalytic critic, Shoshanna Felman, "is always, in fact, to deny it. However one represents madness to oneself or others, to represent madness is always, consciously or unconsciously, to play out the scene of the denial of one's own madness."[55] Yet literary

---

[55] Shoshana Felman, *Writing and Madness*, trans. M. N. Evans and B. Massani (Ithaca, NY and New York: Cornell University Press, 1985) 252.

texts, as she explains, have a complicated relation to the world of madness. If madness is in some sense recognisable by its silence, or lack of intelligible language, then the challenge writers face if they are to give madness a voice is to enact the encounter between speaking about madness and enacting madness. "Writing madness" unsettles and blurs the boundaries between madness as a symptom of the loss of the power to communicate meaningfully and madness as a metaphor for some state of mind or belief that the writer may wish to exclude or excommunicate.

Newman's conflicting desires, both to represent to himself the close relationship to insanity he fears, and yet expel it altogether as a possible inheritance, results in his playing fast and loose with the cause of Juba's madness. It is hinted both that Juba may have inherited his mother's temperament, whereas Agellius was programmed to follow his father's faith, *and* that Juba's problems stem from the accidental, or external, cause of his mother's black magic. (Neither the novel, nor, I think, nineteenth-century medical science indicate any understanding of latent epilepsy as capable of being triggered by some accidental cause).

The unsettling blurring of symptom and metaphor manifests itself in a character who can both be written about as a gibbering, bestial lunatic and be required to carry the scapegoat burden of the Newman brothers' remarkable but "untrustworthy" intellectual capacity. In Juba Newman managed to bypass the perils of the intellect almost entirely. Though we hear much of Juba's "pride of intellect" he is permitted none of the troubling, combative, rationalist discourse that, in Charles Robert's case, continued obdurate against all his brother's "twenty-four closely-worked foolscap pages" and John's attempts on the comfortable fastness of Charles's Tenby exile. Nor is brother Juba permitted to live on in Sicca as a high-minded theist, constituting the kind of public reproach that Frank's appointment to the London Chair must sometimes have seemed. Instead, by miraculous means Juba is deprived of the power of rational discourse, made "quiet, harmless, and silent; the evil spirit had gone out; but he was an idiot."

The overt purpose of the conclusion of Newman's fable was doubtless to show that God alone could restore Juba's intellect and subdue it to the demands of faith. The subtext, however, offers a slightly different gloss. By projecting his fear of the intellect's fragility onto "the other," in the form of a brother, Newman had once again dared to look into the mirror and view himself. Nevertheless the final reconciliation in mature belief that takes place between the faith of Agellius and the, now purified, intellect of Juba could only be safely imagined by deferring it to life beyond the grave, where, as Gerontius was later to express it, he would feel a "sense/ Of freedom, as I were at length myself,/ And ne'er had been before."[56]

---

[56] It is perhaps not without interest that the final verse of *The Dream of Gerontius*, has the Angel, with little obvious theological justification, address Gerontius fraternally:

Farewell, but not for ever, brother dear,
   Be brave and patient on thy bed of sorrow;
Swiftly shall pass thy night of trial here,
   And I will come and wake thee on the morrow. See, *The Dreams*, ll. 897-900.

NOTES ON CONTRIBUTORS

Bruno Forte is Professor of Theology at the Pontifical Faculty of Theology in Naples. His books include *Simbolica Ecclesiale* (8 vols., 1981-96).

Gerard J. Hughes, SJ is master of Campion Hall, Oxford. His books include *The Nature of God* (1995) and *Routledge Philosophy Guide to Aristotle on Ethics* (2001).

Elisabeth Jay is Professor of English at Oxford Brookes University. Her books include *The Religion of the Heart: Anglican Evangelicalism and the Nineteenth-century Novel* (1979), *Faith and Doubt in Victorian England* (1986), and *Mrs. Oliphant: 'A Fiction to Herself': A Literary Life* (1995).

Ian Ker teaches theology at Oxford. His books include the critical edition of *An Essay in Aid of a Grammar of Assent* (1985), *John Henry Newman: A Biography* (1988), and *The Catholic Revival in English Literature, 1845-1961* (2003).

Gerard Loughlin is Senior Lecturer in Religious Studies at the University of Newcastle upon Tyne. He is the author of *Telling God's Story: Bible, Church and Narrative Theology* (1996) and *Alien Sex: Desire and the Body in Cinema and Theology* (2003).

Terrence Merrigan is Professor of Theology at the Catholic University of Leuven. He is the author of *Clear Heads and Holy Hearts: The Religious and Theological Ideal of John Henry Newman* (1990) and editor of *The Myriad Christ: Plurality and the Quest for Unity in Contemporary Christology* (2000).

D. Z. Phillips is Danforth Professor of Philosophy of Religion at Claremont Graduate University. His books include *Philosophy's Cool Place* (1999), *Recovering Religious Concepts* (2000), and *Religion and the Hermeneutics of Contemplation* (2001).

Geoffrey Wainwright is Cushman Professor of Christian theology at Duke University. His books include *Doxology: The Praise of God in Worship, Doctrine and Life* (1980) and *For our Salvation: Two Approaches to the Work of Christ* (1977).

INDEX OF NAMES

Achaval, H.M. de, 98
Allon, Henry, 166
Alston, W.P., 14, 25
Altizer, Thomas J.J., 29
Ambrose, Saint, 90, 156
Aquinas, St. Thomas, 41, 63-64, 67, 77, 89
Aristotle, 2, 55-62, 65-67, 69, 71, 77
Artz, Johannes, 79, 83
Athanasius, Saint, 44, 83, 89, 90
Augustine, St., 28, 75, 79, 89, 112, 124
Austin, J.L. 6

Barrett, Cyril, 185
Barth, Karl, 28, 154
Bentham, Jeremy, 73
Bernard, Saint, 89, 90
Bowden, Mrs. J.W., 163, 168, 169
Bradley, Denis, 63-64
Brodie, Benjamin, 198
Brownlow, W.R., 174
Butler, Bishop Joseph, 2, 146, 148, 175, 189-190

Callista, 198-208
Cameron, James M., 1, 7, 8, 9, 10, 18, 20-21
Caswall, Edward, 95
Chadwick, Owen, 91, 187, 189
Chardin, Teilhard de, 150
Chesterton, G.K., 141
Christie, Lydia Rose, 158, 161
Coleridge, Henry James, 179

Collins, James, 2, 3, 4, 21, 22, 23
Congar, Yves M.J., 178
Copeland, W.J., 166
Copernicus, Nicolaus, 28
Cupitt, Don, 29, 39, 40-42, 47
Cyprian of Carthage, Saint, 157, 201-203

Darwin, Charles, 28, 58
Derrida, Jacques, 39
Descartes, René, 2
Dessain, C.S., 95, 96
Dickens, Charles, 187
Dodsworth, William, 178
Döllinger, Ignaz, 124, 125, 131-132,

Eagleton, Terry, 36, 37
Eliot, T.S., 153, 188
Ellacombe, H.T., 170

Felman, Shoshanna, 206-207
Feuerbach, Ludwig, 29, 30, 39, 42
Fielding-Hall, Harold, 44, 45
Finnis, John, 53-74
Freud, Sigmund, 28, 29, 34
Froude, Catherine, 170
Froude, Richard Hurrell, 119
Froude, William, 2

Galileo, Galilei, 28
Gaskin, J.C.A., 9
Gerontius, 184-185, 208
Gilley, Sheridan, 188, 196
Gladstone, William, 54, 61, 73-74,

157, 159
Gordon, John Joseph, 198
Gunton, Colin, 34, 94-95, 111-115

Heelas, Paul, 36
Hegel, G.W.F., 29
Helbert, Magdalene, 158
Hick, John, 98, 154
Hobbes, Thomas, 58
Holmes, J.D., 98
Holmes, Mary, 180
Hume, David, 8-10, 12, 13, 21, 29
Hyman, Gavin, 39

John XXIII, Pope, 131
John Paul II, Pope, 136, 138, 139, 163, 165
Jungmann, Josef Andreas, 153

Kant, Immanuel, 58, 61
Keble, John, 5, 146, 148, 160, 163
Keogh, C.B., 103
Kepler, Johannes, 28
Ker, Ian, 1, 13, 14, 19, 21, 23, 24, 25, 79, 84, 97, 135, 140, 145, 160,
Kierkegaard, Søren, 77,
Knitter, Paul, 154
Küng, Hans, 132, 134-135

Lacan, Jacques, 186-187
Lash, Nicholas, 135
Lefebvre, Archbishop Marcel, 131-132, 134-135,
Leo, Pope St., 131, 137, 138
Lessing, Gotthold Efraim, 75, 76, 77
Lévi-Strauss, Claude, 28
Liddon, Henry Parry, 160
Lisle, Ambrose Phillipps de (see Phillipps, Andrew Lisle)
Lindbeck, George, 39, 43, 44, 45, 46

Locke, John, 2, 5
Lonergan, Bernard, 44
Loughlin, Gerard, 26, 34, 39
Loyola, Saint Ignatius, 90
Lubac, Henri de, 167
Luther, Martin, 154
Lyotard, J.P., 10, 34, 37

MacIntyre, Alasdair, 36
Manning, Cardinal, 135
Marx, Karl, 28, 29
Mercier, Désiré Cardinal, 33
Merrigan, Terrence, 25, 98, 99, 100, 101, 105, 140
Milbank, John, 28, 29, 39, 43, 46, 47
Milman, Henry Hart, 146, 152, 156, 175
Min, Anselm, 24
Möhler, Johannes Adam, 78
Mounce, H.D., 9, 12-13, 15
Mozley, John Rickards, 157
Mozley, Mrs. John, 143, 161

Nazianzen, Saint Gregory, 89
Newbigin, Lesslie, 155, 161
Newman, Charles, 190, 195-208
Newman, Francis, 192-208
Newman, Harriet, 198
Newman, Jemima, 143, 148, 151, 161, 201
Newsome, David, 188, 190
Newton, Isaac, 28
Niebuhr, H. Richard, 153
Nietzsche, Friedrich, 29, 39, 42, 50

Oppenheim, Janet, 194, 204

Pailin, David, 97
Paley, William, 3
Pascal, Blaise, 80

Paul VI, Pope, 137, 139
Paul, Saint, 152
Penelhum, Terrence, 9
Penny, W.G., 169
Peter, Maude, 25
Philbin, William, 27
Philips, D.Z., 3, 11, 14, 17, 22
Phillipps, Ambrose Lisle, 149, 158, 158, 161, 179
Pickstock, Catherine, 28
Pius IX, Pope, 123, 126
Plantinga, Alvin, 11
Price, Henry Habberly, 96
Pusey, E.B., 145, 158, 159, 160, 164

Quick, Oliver, 167

Rahner, Karl, 115-116, 155, 159
Reding, Charles, 156, 169, 205
Reid, Thomas, 12, 19
Rhees, Rush, 17, 22
Robbins, William, 193
Rogers, Frederic, 122, 164
Rose, Hugh James, 179
Rosmini, Antonio 78
Ryder, George, 151

Sagovsky, Nicholas, 25, 32
St. John, Ambrose, 200
Sanseverino, Gaetano, 77
Saussure, Ferdinand de, 28
Schillebeeckx, Edward, 181
Seeley, John, 146
Sobry, Paul, 108
Socrates, 23
Southey, Robert, 143
Spielberg, Steven, 38

Stephen, James, 144
Stout, Jeffrey, 36
Strange, Roderick, 93,
Svaglic, Martin, 148,
Swinburne, Richard, 2

Taylor, Mark C., 29, 39, 40-42
Taylor, J.P., 165
Thomas, Stephen, 122,
Tierney, Michael, 27
Tillman, Mary Katherine, 101
Tulloch, John, 50
Tyrrell, George, 25, 32, 33

Van Buren, Paul, 29
Vincent of Lerins, 88-89

Wainwright, Geoffrey, 151, 166, 170
Walgrave, J.H., 98
Warburton, William, 29
Ward, Graham, 28, 48
Ward, Wilfred, 25, 32
Ward, Mrs. Wilfred, 32
Warnock, Mary, 98
Weber, Max, 28
Wesley, John, 143, 144, 162, 166
Wilberforce, Henry, 169
Wilberforce, Robert 163
Wilberforce, Samuel, 175, 176
Wiseman, Nicholas, 119
Wittgenstein, Ludwig, 6, 10, 14-15, 16-17, 18, 19, 24, 44, 68
Wright, Terry, 25, 26, 27, 28, 33

Yandell, Keith, 9

Zeno, Dr., 9

INDEX OF SUBJECTS

analogy, 146, 148
Anglicanism, 121, 122, 143, 144, 158, 164, 176, 179
antecedent presumption, 9, 10, 11
antecedent probability, 2-24,
apologetics (negative), 11, 12 24
apologetics (popular), 13
apophaticism, 156
apprehension (see real apprehension; notional apprehension)
Arianism 117-119, 121, 140-141
argument from design, 22
assent, 5, 81 (see also real assent; notional assent)
atonement, 157

Berkeleyism, 148
Branch Theory of the church, 125, 158, 162

capitalism, 37
Catechism of the Catholic Church, 70
certainty, 1
certitude, 2-7, 12
Chalcedon, Council of, 121, 131, 170
christology, 93
conscience, 20-21, 32, 53-74, 104-105
consubstantiality, 44
cosmology, 34
creation, 34

Darwinism, 34
death of God (theology of), 29
deconstructionism, 40

development of doctrine (see doctrine)
Dissenters, 143
docetism, 150
doctrine, 44-46, 75-92, 93-116, 120, 121, 132-142, 143, 146-147, 149, 152, 153, 163, 173-175,
dogma, 31, 51, 83, 95, 102-111, 123-132, 155, 159, 170; see also infallibility; ecumenical councils

ecumenical councils, 117-142
empiricism, 2, 6, 8, 9, 10, 97
Erastianism, 121
euthanasia, 70
evangelization, 138

faith, 34, 51, 55, 93-116,
Fall, 34
Fideism, 51
foundationalism, 51-52

Gallicanism, 125
grand narratives (see master stories)

heresy, 122, 123,
hermeneutic circle, 90
hermeneutics, 81, 90, 91

idea of Christianity, 27, 32, 133-142
Idealism, 148, 150
illative sense, 4, 7, 12, 53-74
imagination, 21, 31, 97-98, 106, see also 'religious imagination'
incarnation, 141, 144, 167, 169, 181

infallibility, 32, 53-74, 88, 123-142, 164-166

Jansenism, 125
justification, 172-180

laity, 138-142
language games, 19,
Liberalism, 30-31, 32, 50-51
Liberal Catholicism, 25, 134,
liberal theology, 30-31, 118
Louvain, 73

Marxism, 34
Mary, Blessed Virgin, 138
master stories / narratives, 34, 35, 36
metaphor, 26
metaphysics, 30, 82
Methodism, 143-145, 162
Modernism (Catholic), 25, 27, 31, 32, 33
modernism (cultural), (see modernity)
modernism (theological), 29
modernity, 25-52, 78, 85
Monophysites, 121, 122
movements, new ecclesial, 138-142
mystery, 106-107, 111, 147, 174

narrativity, 43, 45-50
naturalism, 12, 24
nature of things (principle of), 8
negative theology, 48
Neo-Scholasticism, 77
Nicaea, Council of, 44, 117, 118, 122,
Nonconformists, 166
Nonjurors, 143, 144,
notional apprehension, 95-96, 99-111, 114
notional assent, 95-96, 99-111, 114

Old Catholics, 131
orthodoxy (doctrinal), 47
Oxford Movement, 119; see also Tractarianism; Tract 90

pantheism, 150
papacy, 27, 123-133, 135, 137; see also infallibility;
philosophy, 23-24, 38, 40, 133, 134, 145, 148, 152,
phronēsis, 53-74
postmodernism / postmodernity, 25-52
post-structuralism, 40
probability, 2-4, 6-8
probabilism, 73
Protestantism, 81, 119, 122, 148-149, 154, 161, 162
psychologism, 5-8, 20, 24

Radical Orthodoxy, 28
real apprehension, 94-111, 114
real assent, 6, 20, 21, 94-111, 114
Real Presence, 16, 149; see also 'transubstantiation'
reception, theory of, 124-142
redemption, 34
Reformation (Protestant), 28, 176, 179
Reformed epistemology, 10
relativism, 81
religious imagination 29, 31, 52, 94, 96-99
Romanticism, 97

sacramental principle 145, 146-156
sacramental system, 21, 143-182
secular theology, 29
solipsism, 6
Sophists, 23
structuralism, 40

theology, Liberal, see Liberal theology
theology, negative (see negative theology)
theology, science of, 102-103, 129-130
Tract 90, 121, 149, 176
Tractarianism, 120, 122
tradition, 27, 73, 119, 120
transubstantiation, 11, 149
Trent, Council of, 118, 119, 120, 121, 128, 136,
Trinity, 93-116

Ultramontanism, 123-124, 125, 131-132
utilitarianism, 58, 65

Vatican Council I, 117-142
Vatican Council II, 127-142, 154
via media, theory of, 79-80, 119, 120, 122, 134,

Wesleyanism, 145
world pictures, 18-19, 22, 23, 24

PRINTED ON PERMANENT PAPER • IMPRIME SUR PAPIER PERMANENT • GEDRUKT OP DUURZAAM PAPIER - ISO 9706

N.V. PEETERS S.A., WAROTSTRAAT 50, B-3020 HERENT